AGENTS OF PEACE MINISTERS OF CONFLICT

Basic Training in the Resolution of Conflicts for Local Churches

LEVEL 1: BASIC TRAINING CURRICULUM

INSTRUCTOR'S MANUAL

MICHAEL W. DEWAR, SR.

Published in the United States by:
Dwelling Place Cleansing
PO Box 360196
Brooklyn, New York 11236

ISBN: 978-1-7334377-5-2

Scripture quotations are generally taken from the New International Version (NIV) Copyright © 1973, 1978, 1984, 2011 by International Bible Society. Used by permission. All rights reserved. Where other sources are used, the acronym of the translation is indicated (e.g. KJV, NKJV, ESV).

CONTENTS

PREFACE

This book is written to be used in conjunction with the textbook, *CHURCH AND FAMILY CONFLICTS: How to Settle Conflicts Peacefully in the House* by Michael W. Dewar, Sr. This is the instructor's version of the curriculum; there is also a *Student Manual* version, each sold separately. The instructor needs this curriculum manual and the textbook when teaching this course of study.

The course can be completed in six weeks by attending a 4 to 5-hour class one day each week. When done this way, students will commence reading the textbook two weeks ahead, before the first day of class, and continue doing the assigned reading to the end of the course of study. However, churches, schools, and ministry agencies can adjust the time schedule to suit their own purposes.

A WORD FROM THE AUTHOR

Dear Ministry Colleague,

Welcome to an exciting and transformative course of study in the management and resolution of conflict for the local church; in short, peacemaking. Without question, this course worths the investment of your time and money. It helps to preserve ministry legacy and good name for decades to come; it does not allow destructive conflict to destroy years of hard work. God does not want the pastor in the hearth of every conflict. You don't have to attend or preside over every fight; ministry is not the referee business. This course empowers you and your church to become a peace-loving, peacemaking church. Your first challenge is to get your members to participate in the training.

This study evolves out of years of experience shepherding God's people and working with pastors. I am convinced that destructive conflict is, perhaps, the greatest hinderance to the flourishing of the local church. It fractures unity and hinders churches from fulfilling their mission to the community and the world. In short order, conflict can destroy the work of a lifetime, leaves you suffering from burnout, ruins your health, shreds your reputation and sends you packing.

Many pastors have made the colossal mistake, thinking it can't happen to them, until the chant from the pews change from "Hosanna" to Crucify him!" By then, it is almost too late to salvage anything. The autopsy of most dead churches and ministries reveal that their death and dying were not that dramatic, but they end up dead, nonetheless. This course is intended to lead you and your church far from that paralyzing and tragic path of death and dying to flourishing.

To teach this course, you will need at least one or two committed instructors with yourself. Two of your best lay persons will do just fine. The instructors and planners should review the last three lessons (18,19 and 20) early in the planning stage so you can know the end from the beginning.

Training your people to practice their Christian duties of peacemaking and peacekeeping is a great ministry investment. Stress attendance, punctuality, reading ahead in the textbook and reading assignments. By the first day of class they should have read the introduction and chapter one of the textbook. Give a short quiz (five questions) on the assigned reading every time the class meets (see examples in appendix B). Keep a record of the scores for each student. May the blessed Holy Spirit give you success!

Pastor Michael W. Dewar, M.Div., LMSW, D.MIN

INTRODUCTION

This curriculum is designed to be used with the main textbook, *Church and Family Conflict* by the same author. It is the textbook of choice when conducting training to launch a peace ministry at the local church. The curriculum follows the textbook and is based upon the author's Regent University doctoral dissertation, a more technical research document in church conflict.

This *Basic Training* edition comes in two versions: The instructor's version and the Student's Manual version. Be sure to note the distinction at time of purchase. The primary textbook required for the course is, *Church and Family Conflicts: How to Settle Them in the House* by Michael W. Dewar, Sr. Available on *Amazon* and other places where books are sold. Use the paperback edition.

Jesus said, "Blessed are the peacemakers, for they will be called children of God" (Matt. 5:9). From this and other scripture passages, it is clear that peacemaking is a Christian duty, and the Lord of the Church expects His followers to be agents of peace. A good agent must have the knowledge and the skills necessary to manage and resolve conflicts effectively, so the agent of peace is also manager.

All true believers are called to "seek peace and pursue it" (Ps. 34:14, Heb. 12:14). This suggests that the duty of peacemaking has to be supplemented by the duty of peacekeeping. It is further evident from scripture that Jesus the Prince of peace, is the supreme example all believers should strive to emulate. The scripture further established that the church cannot effectively fulfills its mission to itself, the community and the world, if her unity is fractured by conflict and she is at war with herself.

In His High Priestly prayer, Jesus prayed for the unity of the church. The quality of unity He desires for the church is likened to the unity that binds together the persons of the blessed Holy Trinity as One God (John 17:20). Has the church achieved a semblance of this unity? The evidence shows that the church has not even come close; a culture of conflict exists in many local churches, preventing them from fulfilling their mission assignment of evangelizing the world and making disciples (Matt. 28:19-20).

The scripture further reveals that where destructive conflict prevails, there is a shortage of love for God and neighbor. It is the desire of Jesus Christ that His Church be a community of faith marked by love (John 13:34-35). This curriculum seeks to equip members of the local church to become agents of peace and managers of conflict; it seeks to establish a dedicated lay ministry for peace at the local church under the day to day direction of a *Resident Counsel* (RC) and with pastoral oversight.

The *Agents of Peace-Managers of Conflict* curriculum (APMC) is a biblical approach to the resolution of conflict. It is intended to train believers to be true agents of peace, to develop their Christian duties of peacemaking and peacekeeping from a biblical perspective, to preserve the unity of the church, and to guard the integrity of its message and mission to the community and the world.

The curriculum pulls together ten (10) general themes on conflict resolution and ten (10) biblical themes specific to peacemaking. The manager of conflict is expected to show understanding and competence in these twenty (20) themes that constitute the core of this Basic Training. In this study, competence is viewed as the mastery of a prescribed body of knowledge on the one hand, and spiritual formation or character on the other hand. Jesus Christ is the supreme example Christians seek to emulate; therefore, knowledge and Christlikeness are combined in this pursuit.

The training specifically equips members of the local church to be agents of peace. The church will then choose five to seven (5-7) of the trained agents of peace to serve on a *Resident Counsel* (RC) as managers of conflict, depending of the size of your church. The RC is the peace ministry rapid response team based at the local church.

The RC for a small to medium-size church needs no more than five to six members, a large church 7-8, and a megachurch 8-12 at most. It is strongly recommended to get as many members as possible to complete the *Basic Training* course of study. They can form a pool from which to draw persons to fill vacancies on the counsel. *Counsel m*embers may have term limit of three years. All members of the church are part of the peace ministry; it is their Christian duty. But the counsel is the formal ministry tasked to serve as the rapid response peacekeeping force of the church.

A Tri-phasic Curriculum

This is a forward-looking curriculum of three levels or phases. Phase 1: Basic Training: Becoming an Agent of Peace-Manager of Conflict—has twenty (20) lessons. It is strongly recommended that you train as many members as possible for this level, so you can have a pool of 10-20 people left after you have chosen 5-7 persons for your peace ministry team or Resident Counsel. Another reason for the pool is—you may not be able to repeat the Basic Training every year.

Phase 2: *Intermediate Training Curriculum*, has fifteen (15) lessons. This level of training is designed to increase the skills and competence of those who have successfully completed the basic training. Only graduates from the basic training phase can be admitted to this Level 2 Training.

Phase 3: *Advanced Training Curriculum* is for prospective instructors. It has fifteen (15) lessons. Only persons that have completed Levels 1 and 2 can be admitted to Level 3. People that successfully complete this level can teach the course in their church as well as other churches.

Lessons and Assignments

Again, there are nineteen (19) lessons in *Basic Training*. They can be completed in six-weeks, meeting for four hours (4) of instruction once each week (i.e. six class days of four hours each). Each lesson can be completed in one hour (includes 5-10 minutes break).

Planners can also use other creative time schedule to match the need of their particular church. Some churches try to get it done in a three or four-day retreat; that would require extensive textbook reading weeks before the retreat. When following the six-week schedule, an extra two hours may be necessary at the closing end for review and evaluation (R&R). Review covers the highlights of the course in preparation for the long quiz or final exam, as some like to call it. Trying to fit all the lessons in a section in one four-hour class day is a daunting process and is much advised against. Rushing through the training is counterproductive.

Students will have sequentially assigned readings to accomplish at home every day leading up to the class sessions. Instructors will emphasize the importance of these assigned readings. A short quiz of five (5} questions covering the assigned readings, will be given each day of class. The score received on the short quiz will be counted toward the student's final grade (see sample syllabus in appendix A).

It cannot be overemphasized that doing the reading assignments is an integral part of the course. Therefore, to successfully complete the course, students must diligently do the assigned readings, attend class, and engaged in class participation (i.e. short quiz, class discussion, the final test).

All persons successfully completing the course will be awarded a certificate. These individuals may go on to the second and third phases of the training when offered. Those not successful, may repeat the course when it is offered again.

In order to evaluate each student accurately at the ending of the course, the instructors must keep accurate attendance record, short quiz score, assignment completion, class participation and final exam scores. Some members who have been out of school for decades will be taking the course, so the scoring system is quite flexible and generous, so even the below average student that does the work should be able to successfully complete the course.

INSTRUCTOR'S NOTES

_____

_____

_____

_____

_____

_____

_____

_____

_____

_____

_____

_____

_____

_____

_____

_____

_____

_____

SECTION I
BECOMING AN AGENT OF PEACE

OVERVIEW

The focus of Section I is on you the practitioner, herein called, the *Agent of Peace*. As a disciple of Christ, the Lord has already designated you an agent of peace; that is exactly who a peacemaker is. If you are not an agent of peace, you are an agent of something else and your spiritual paternity is in question because peacemakers are called, "children of God" ((Matt.5:9).

To be an effective agent of peace, you must acquire the knowledge and skills to *manage conflicts* and bring them to resolution. That is exactly what this course is about; it equips you to manage and resolve conflicts effectively. Becoming an effective agent of peace-manager of conflict is a process; you work at it to develop competence.

You are called to be an agent of peace for Christ and His church; it is a special ministry. The Prince of peace is Jesus and His enterprise or business is the Church. Jesus is not here in the flesh, but you are! And you are His agent. To be a good peace agent, you must know the person you represent (Jesus), know yourself well (the agent), and know the people you serve (the church). Proper spiritual formation normally produces an authentic vision of God, self, and people (Isa.6:1-8).

There are five lessons in section one: 1) The need for a conflict management plan, 2) Your preferred way of dealing with conflict, 3) Your theology of conflict, 4) Peace as a Christian duty, and 5) Why churches need to manage conflict effectively. Be sure to inform students to always read ahead in the textbook, completing the reading assignments. It makes things easier for instructor and students.

Have student's do the exercise, *My Conflict Style*, in Appendix B of student manual in preparation for Lesson 2. The exercise has no right or wrong answer. They should prepare to share their discovery in Lesson 2 class session.

Instructor's Notes:

_____
_____
_____
_____
_____
_____
_____
_____
_____
_____
_____
_____
_____
_____
_____
_____
_____
_____

FIRST DAY OF CLASS

Welcome and Introduction

- Pastor welcomes the students and introduces the other instructors assisting her or him.

- Emphasize the importance of the study to the success of the overall ministry of the church.

- Show that no house or kingdom divided against itself can stand, that conflict divides and defeats the church in its mission assignment to the community and the world.

- With an established peace ministry, we learn to manage and resolve conflicts to the glory of God

State the Purpose of this Course of Study

- To equip the members of this church to live out their Christian duties of peacemaking and peacekeeping at home, at church, and in the marketplaces of this world.

- To prepare our church to launch its own resident peace ministry as a system to manage and resolve situations of conflict before they become destructive to our mission and purpose.

- To preserve the unity of our church and prevent conflict from derailing its mission.

Review syllabus with Students (See Appendix A)

- Emphasize class attendance and punctuality.
- Emphasize completing assignments in a timely manner.

- Emphasize what is needed to receive a certificate of completion: regular attendance, completion of assignments, passing score on quizzes and final exams.
- Emphasize that scoring is flexible and generous so anyone that does the work should be able to successfully complete the course.

Prayer of Blessing and Enablement
- Be sure to begin each day or teaching session with prayer.

- Be sure to end the day or session with prayer.

Instructor's Notes:

_____
_____
_____
_____
_____
_____
_____
_____
_____
_____
_____
_____
_____
_____
_____
_____
_____
_____
_____
_____
_____
_____

LESSON 1

THE NEED FOR A PEACE PLAN

Reading Assignment: (Textbook: Read Introduction and Chapter 1)

Lesson Focus and Purpose

This lesson addresses the "why" of this training. The research literature has not lied, a culture of conflict indeed prevails in many of our local churches, derailing them from effectively carrying out their assigned mission. Furthermore, no church is immune from the destructive power of conflict; it fractures unity, pits member against member, sabotages leadership, and compromises the integrity of its message.

Unlike secular organizations, most churches have no dedicated peace ministry or mechanism to manage and resolve conflicts. They do not even have a grievance committee, so simple disagreements or dissatisfactions become distorted, develop into gossips and take on a disruptive life of their own.

Every business enterprise of significance has a conflict management system (CMS), but not the church. The fact is, we do not take conflict seriously until we are in a crisis. This is the reality of thousands of local churches. We are here to examine this lackadaisical attitude toward the reality of conflict and render a workable solution. *Each one of us will become a solution to destructive conflict, not the cause of it* (repeat that with me). Declare to yourself today, that you are an agent of peace.

Undoubtedly, this lack of an intentional system to resolve conflict, is one compelling reason local churches need a strategic peace plan. *But what is your personal why?* Conflict at home? Conflict at work? Each of you in a sentence or two, share with this class your "why" for wanting to take this course on the *resolution of conflict and peacemaking.*

Lesson Content Issues to Emphasize

Discuss the following statements? (from the introduction of the Textbook):

- In relation to the church, "Effective ministering and organizational survival demand a proactive conflict management and resolution plan" or system.

- The way most churches respond to conflict is: "They wait until they are in a crisis, then they have a panic reaction" (an approach that is almost always disastrous).

- A dispute resolution system is urgently needed because each day "new conflicts are emerging from the shadows, including sexual harassment and domestic violence. These scandals are toppling business leaders, resulting in millions of dollars in settlement and litigation cost. They also derail the organizations from their mission and purpose."

- Should church scandal be played out in the public square and social media, or should the church have a system to manage dispute internally and control its message to the public? In other word, should churches hang out their dirty laundry for the world to hear and see?

Some Reasons Churches Have Not Done Better Managing Conflict

- Conflict management training is a recent inclusion in ministry education.

- Conflict management training usually targets professional clergy at the master's and doctorate levels. It is not generally an area of concentration in seminary or divinity school; other than a few exceptions, it is limited to just a few courses.
- Christian conflict education has not sufficiently filtered down to persons in the pews of local churches, because in most cases, it requires a bachelor's degree to access, many lay persons cannot afford tuition payment, some have no computer skills, and the obligation of work and family compound the difficulty.
- Peace education is not historically a priority of the local church; they hardly budget for it.

If the community of faith cannot be at peace with itself, then the chance to win the larger community to Christ is lost. If pastors, deacons and members are the negative talk of the town, then the water is already poison. The church must first reflect the alternative culture of the kingdom of God to the community in order to be a positive impact on it and its people.

Lesson Application

I trust you are beginning to see the need for a peace ministry at the local church and why you need to be a part of it. We have surveyed few of the causes to the existence of the culture of conflict at the local church; we have not explored them all. But like the author of our textbook, do you agree that the need for a plan to remedy the situation is urgent? Urgency calls for immediate action to fix a problem.

That plan to fix the problem begins with each of us acquiring the skills to be agent of peace and a manager of conflict. When you see a conflict in your church about to get out of hand, don't walk away and say, it's not my business. It is your business, so do something!

Remind student to do the exercise, *My Conflict Style*, in Appendix B of student manual in preparation for Lesson 2. The exercise has no right or wrong answer. Students should prepare to share their discovery in Lesson 2 class session.

Instructor's Notes:

_____

_____

_____

_____

_____

_____

_____

_____

_____

_____

_____

_____

_____

_____

_____

_____

_____

_____

_____

_____

_____

LESSON 2

DISCOVERING YOUR CONFLICT STYLE

Reading Assignment: (Read Textbook: Review CH.1)

Exercise Assignment: Do at home the exercise in "Appendix B" of the student manual and be prepared to share your discoveries in class.

Lesson Purpose

This lesson helps you to develop insight into your own conflict style or discover what your conflict style is. Wittingly or unwittingly, each person has a preferred way of dealing with conflict but most of us don't think about it. It is commonly called, your *preferred conflict style*. Identifying that style, helps you learn about yourself, so that you can intentionally shape that style to work for you and learn new ones.

Lesson Content Issues to Emphasize

In Chapter 1 of the textbook seven conflict styles are mentioned (confronting, accommodating, rationalizing, negotiating or bargaining, collaborating, avoidance, persuading). In the first half of this class session briefly review these with your students. Have each student write down the style he or she most frequently use when responding to conflict. Six of the seven are listed below but not exactly.

Consciously or unconsciously, each one of us use at least one of the seven or six as our preferred way of responding to conflict, so it is labeled our *preferred conflict style*. That means our personality gravitates to one or more of these patterns when we are in conflict with another person or persons.

In the second half of the class, review the exercise in *"Appendix B"* of the student manual that each student did at home. Each student will share which of the six styles he or she identifies as his or her *conflict style (*i.e. the style with the highest score). Also note the second highest score.

1. Persuading (Confronting)
2. Compelling
3. Accommodating/Avoiding
4. Collaborating
5. Negotiating
6. Support

Now, compare the exercise results with what each student had previously written down. Does your perception of your conflict style come close to the results you got on the exercise? Don't get emotional about it; it's just an exercise to give you insight on how you respond to conflict. So, which of the six conflict responses is most closely associated with you? Have each student shares his or her score with the class. Which columns have the highest and second highest scores for you? Those are the two styles you are like to use in a conflict. They are neither good nor bad, if they work for you.

By the end of this course, you want to be proficient in many ways to respond to conflict. You don't want to be locked into just one or two ways.

Lesson Application

Whatever your conflict settlement style may be, you can intentionally shape a multi-prong approach that can serve you well now and in years to come. As an agent of peace, to manager conflict effectively, you need a diversified toolkit and you must constantly upgrade your competence in the use of each tool.

Perhaps, our next lesson, *You Theology of Peace,* is the best place for the Christian peace agent to begin because it helps you to consciously hammer out your personal theology of conflict. It has to be anchored in scripture and reflects the peace theology of Jesus in regard to violence, war and peace. Jesus did not come to us on a war horse, but as a baby in a manger. That is a symbol of peace and the serenading angels confirmed it with their song of peace (Luke 2:9-14).

Instructor's Notes:

_____

_____

_____

_____

_____

_____

_____

_____

_____

_____

_____

_____

_____

_____

_____

_____

LESSON 3

YOUR THEOLOGY OF CONFLICT

Reading Assignment: (Textbook: Review the theology of Jesus in Ch.1 and read Ch.2)

Scripture Reading: (Matthew 5-7 the Sermon on the Mount)

Lesson Purpose

Theology of conflict is the same as theology of peace, the terms are used interchangeably. This lesson shows that human attitude toward conflict, violence, war and peace is largely driven by their humanistic philosophy or worldview, that includes the holy war or just war theory. On the contrary, God wants the attitudes of His children to reflect the attitude of His Son toward violence and war. That attitude is referred to in this study as the *peace theology of Jesus*. It shapes His entire ministry on earth but is extensively reflected in His Sermon on the Mount (Matt.5-7).

As a child of God, you are a peace agent of Jesus Christ. You too need a peace theology or theology of peace that is anchored in Scripture, that conforms to Jesus' attitude toward violence and war and reflects the very nature of God. To do so biblically, you must pay close attention to the theology of Jesus which comes out clearly in the Sermon on the Mount as well as in His entire life on earth. He was the Prince of peace.

Lesson Contents

- **What is a peace theology or theology of peace?** A peace theology is a personal guiding principle anchored in the word of God that governs our behavior in the face of conflict, violence and war.

- **Theology versus Philosophy**: theology is rooted in God and scripture. Philosophy is a human ideology based upon opinions and logic as a guiding principle for living.

- **Discussion**: Did Jesus have a peace theology, a preferred way of dealing with conflict? (*Instructor's answer*: Yes, it is reflected in the Sermon on the Mount and His total ministry lifestyle on earth). By life, character and practice, Jesus was the Man of peace.

Furthermore, the peace theology of Jesus is boldly reflected in His new command to love God and neighbor. He commands us to put away our sword of violence, not to perpetuate violence by demanding an "eye for an eye and a tooth for tooth," but turn the other cheek and go the extra mile, to love our enemies, and pray for those that despised and abused us (Matt.5:38-41,43-48). Emphasize Jesus' New Commandment, the law of love (What is this consisted of?):

1. A higher standard of righteousness based upon the primacy of love for God and neighbor (Matt.5:20; John13:34-35; Mark 12:30-32). This new standard of righteousness requires the peaceful resolution of conflicts (Matt.5:38-45). Neighbor is redefined to mean all your fellow human beings; all bear the Imago Dei (image of God).

1. (See preceding higher standard of righteousness)

2. The new standard of righteousness teaches that obedience motivated by love is better than sacrifice. Obedience motivated by love is stronger and more desirable than obedience out of fear of punishment. When the threat of punishment wears off, people tend to return to their native habits. It's like an elastic band that retracks to its normal size when the pressure is off.

3. Obedience motivated by love requires a changed heart. The Old Covenant by itself could not give people a changed heart because it was weak (Rom.8:3-4).

4. The new standard of righteousness motivated by love for God and neighbor is possible because the New Covenant was forged with God's law written inwardly by the Holy Spirit (Jer.31:31-34; Heb.8:7-13). The letter kills but the Spirit gives life.

5. How did God model His new standard of righteousness? He became man in the person of Jesus Christ (John 1:1-2,14). Jesus is the personified standard of God's righteousness; this righteousness is imputed to all believers. Under the New Covenant, retributive justice (vengeance) is partly retained by God and partly given to the ministers of secular state to command an orderly society (Heb.10:30; Rom.13:1-8).

Probing Question to the Students:

1. Did the apostles and the early Church practice the peace theology of Jesus Christ? (**Instructor's answer:** Yes, all through the apostolic period which brings us to the end of the first century. And the Church Fathers continued it through most of the Patristic period-that is, from about the ending 100 AD to 450 AD).

2. When did the church depart from the peace theology of Jesus? (Instructor's Answer: During Medieval Papal Rome which runs from about AD 450 to 1500 AD. The papacy sanctioned the brutality of the Crusades and the Inquisitions). The church members were not allowed to read the Bible. With the fall of secular Rome, the Church assumed the power of the state and ruled by the sword.

Lesson Application

How then do we recapture the peace theology of Jesus to formulate and practice our own peace theology? We return to the word of God — the Sermon of the Mount and the early Church. We return to the New Testament and take its contents seriously.

The centrality of the Word of God cannot be overemphasized; it is the final rule for faith and practice for Christian life. The command of Jesus is not, love your friends and family and hate your enemies but love your neighbors, love your enemies, do good to them that despitefully use you (see Matt.5:43-48; John 13:34-35).

As God's agent of peace in this world, we must be willing to put down the sword and work for peace. You may not possess a gun or another instrument of violence, but the tongue has the power of life and death. It is a deadly weapon and it is the starter of most conflicts.

Instructor's Notes:

_____

_____

_____

_____

_____

_____

_____

_____

_____

_____

_____

_____

_____

_____

_____

_____

_____

_____

_____

_____

_____

_____

_____

LESSON 4

PEACE AS A CHRISTIAN DUTY

Reading Assignment: (Read Textbook CH.3)

Lesson Purpose

This lesson shows that being an *Agent of Peace* is not optional for the new life in Christ, if a person truly wants to live in obedience to Christ. Peacemaking is a central requirement, a lifestyle. Being peacemaker is an identifying mark of a true child of God (Matt.5:9). Peacemaking and peacekeeping are Christian duties. This lesson helps the students to come to that understanding and take on that responsibility with a renewed commitment, knowing it is a Christian duty indeed.

Lesson Content

1. Address the question: Why church members are so quick to trash their own church and demonize their own leaders? History reveals that churches do not usually fall apart because of external pressure or persecution. In fact, they thrive better when they are under pressure and pushed to the margins of society. They are more at risk when they are at ease and comfort in society. To answer the question:

- **Emphasize the lack of Education on what church membership is all about is partly responsible.** People are added to the church and they are hardly taught that the church is a Divine Institution unlike any other. It is

God's enterprise (business). It has a mission (Matt.28:19-20). It delivers a product, the Gospel (Rom.1:16-17). It requires commitment and loyalty to Christ and each other to fulfill this mission. Trashing and abandoning one's local church to flee to another (Cross Town church) is anathema.

- **Emphasize the lack of Education on Peacemaking as a Christian duty (Matt.5:9)**. Peacemaking is the business of every member of the church because it is a Christian duty. But most churches talk of peace especially at Christmas time, but members have not been trained how to practice peace as a Christian duty. The practice of peace includes knowledge on how to prevent conflict, how to manage conflict biblically, and how to bring conflicted situation to resolution.

- **Emphasize that Seeking Peace and Pursuing it also a Christian duty (1Peter 3:8-11).** Go after peace, just don't sit back and wait for it to come to you. As much as it depends on you live peaceable with all people (Rom.12:18).

- **Emphasize Peacekeeping as a Christian duty**. Being a peacemaker is not enough. Peacemaking is the effort to bring cessation to hostility or ceasefire; it may even end the war. But there are issues to address to have a sustainable peace. This is why the United Nations has a peacekeeping force. They go in to keep the peace until a lasting peace is negotiated. Christians are called to be peacekeepers. Peacemakers work for peace.

2. Three Big Idea in the Duty of Peace: The ideas in this section will be discussed in detail in later lessons; the instructor may choose not to dwell on them here, just briefly preview them:

- **To achieve peace, you must be willing to work for forgiveness.** That is—if you are the victim, the one that is hurt, you must make the decision to forgive the one who hurts you. If you are the perpetrator you must ask for forgiveness and allow time to grant it.

- **To work toward justice and restitution.** God wants justice to be tempered with mercy. "Blessed are the merciful for they shall obtain mercy" (Matt.5:7). Restitution is giving back what was stolen or taken by fraud. If it cannot be restored, arrange for some form of compensation. In some cases, the defrauded person releases the debt (that is material property). They thief stole your Mercedes from your driveway. You may forgive him by not pressing charges, but that does not mean he gets to keep the Mercedes.

- **To work for reconciliation of relationship or release it.** This is the ideal end goal of forgiveness. But sinful human often fallen short of God's ideal. In some cases, reconciliation of relationship is not achievable. In such cases, you release the relationship. Some examples of such cases are rape, domestic violence, and murder,

Lesson Application

We have seen that the Christian duty of peace is no small thing, that it has several facets to it. The first is peacemaking which is not a onetime event; it is a lifestyle.

Second, we must seek peace and pursue it. Third, the ongoing work of peacekeeping. Peace work requires specialized knowledge and relational skills to manage and resolve conflicted situations. As Agents of peace, our best example is Jesus Christ himself, and our best instruction manual is the Bible itself.

Additional, for members to stop trashing their churches, we need to redefine membership in the context of the nature of the church as a divine institution and the loyalty of its members to Christ by being loyal to His Body.

Instructor's Notes:

_____
_____
_____
_____
_____
_____
_____
_____
_____
_____
_____
_____
_____
_____
_____
_____
_____
_____
_____
_____

LESSON 5

WHY CHURCHES NEED TO MANAGE CONFLICTS EFFECTIVELY

Reading Assignment: (Read textbook Ch.4 and review Ch.3).

Purpose of this Lesson:

This lesson digs deeper into the rationale for a formal, conflict management system (CMS) at the local church. It looks at why such ministry is critical to the purpose and assigned mission of the church.

Lesson Contents Exploration (textbook Ch.3):

1. The Unique Nature of the Church Demands A Conflict Management System

- In the light of Matthew **(16:16-18), discuss w**hat kind of organization the Church is.
- The church is a voluntary organization unlike any other on earth.
- The church is a human and divine entity (It is divine *origin*, *purpose* and *power)*
- The purpose of the church *is* redemptive.

2. The Mission of the Church Warrants A Conflict Management System.

- *The church is a global enterprise with a global mission* (Matt.28:19-20). The church is not the only multi-national, global enterprise (e.g. Apple, GM, IBM) but they all have a temporal, material product to distribute. To do so seamlessly, they must protect their brand and manage conflict effectively.

- *The church has a product to distribute.* That product is the gospel; it is supernatural and redemptive. The mission to evangelize the world is a unified one. Fractured unity or a divided house will hinder its delivery. Jesus wants the highest quality of unity for the church (John 17:9-11,20-21). Furthermore, the Holy Spirit cannot work with discord (Luke 4:14-20, 28-30; Acts 2:1-4). A conflicted sheepfold is not ready to make or nurture disciples.

- *Review five challenges to the mission of the church*: 1) the quality of its unity, 2) malicious discord prevents the work of the Holy Spirit, 3) the practice of love restricted, 4) the health of the congregation and leadership endangered by conflict, 5) the lack of an intentional, dedicated system to manage and resolve conflict.

3. The Work of the Church Compels A Conflict Management System.

The church has two indispensable tasks, apart from them, it has no reason for being:

- *Worship*—there is no greater activity in heaven or earth than worship. It is what God wants and it is what the devil wants (Matt.4:8-10). Satan will pay top dollar to get it. Or, he will demand it by force, at the point of a gun (Rev.13). God set the standard of worship under the old covenant as to how you can approach Him. God is Holy. Wants to be worship in Spirit and in truth (John 4:23-).

- *Disciple-making*—it is the core of the great commission (Matt.28:19-20). Satan will do every think in his power to disrupt and corrupt these two central activities of the church. Nothing corrupts them better than destructive conflict.

Lesson Application

The high quality of unity Jesus wants for His church is the quality of unity that binds the persons of the blessed Holy Trinity as one God. Worship is what the church does, but for it to be accepted in heaven, it must be done in the Holy Spirit (John 4:24). If it is not done in the Spirit, it is done in the flesh and heaven cannot accept it; it is corrupted. Conflict is the chief corrupter. It divides and conquers.

Disciple making is the core mission of the church; nothing hinders that more perfectly than destructive conflict. A family fraught with conflict is dysfunctional and the children that are born and nurtured in that environment are likely to produce dysfunctional families of their own. War and fights, divisions and schisms in churches are all birth out of conflicts (Jas. 4:1-3).

If fire keep burning down your kitchen; at least invest in a fire extinguisher. Each local church needs its own conflict management and resolution system. That is why an inhouse peace ministry is indispensable. "All organizations, Christian and non-Christian, need harmony to function orderly, productively and optimally."

SECTION II

UNDERSTANDING THE DYNAMICS OF CONFLICT

(Lesson 6 to 10)

SECTION II

UNDERSTANDING THE DYNAMICS OF CONFLICT

OVERVIEW

Painting with a broad brush, this section looks at how conflict behaves and how it was responded to by the ancient people of God in both Old and New Testament, as well as throughout the history of the church. The revelation of God to His people is progressive, so perhaps, His word has precedence as to how God wants His people to deal with conflict, violence and war.

Before the Prince of Peace arrived to give us the New Covenant (the New Testament), He casts a long prophetic shadow before Him in the Hebrew Bible (The Old Testament) concern His person, nature and character. God never left humankind in the dark but shows them by what standards He wants them to live. Those standards are revealed in His word and they are precedence that provide insight as to how we must now live as the people of God.

This section, therefore, carries five lesson: one has to do with *A Strategic Peacemaking Plan* and four address the question of precedence in the Old and New Testament and throughout the history of the church. Because the time periods are long and the material voluminous, we paint in broad strokes.

Lesson 9 discusses the Patristic Period and touches upon the Reformation Period. To get some understanding of the Reformation, it is helpful to know something about Martin Luther. Watch this movie on Luther at home by copying and pasting the link in your computer browser. Watch with someone else; for best effects project to a wide screen TV. You can also go to Youtube and search for Luther, the movie, then compare the link with this: https://www.youtube.com/watch?v=_rJwCqhTyY8 . The movie will be much more fun if students get together and watch it in groups or all at once.

LESSON 6

A STRATEGIC PEACEMAKING PLAN

Reading Assignment: (Read Textbook CH.5 and Review CH.4)

Lesson Purpose

We have concluded in previous lessons that the church is a divine enterprise with a global mission and a redemptive product to deliver called, the gospel. To be successful delivering the gospel product, the local church has to be unified, not fragmented by conflict. Unity demands a plan.

This lesson examines what that plan to manage and resolve conflict should look like. A plan used to work for peace and preserve unity, what should it look like? The nature of the enterprise determines the nature of the plan. The church is a spiritual enterprise, much different from Walmart, so its conflict resolution templet has to be guided by spiritual values or a spiritual manual or handbook. In this case, the Bible.

Lesson Content (Emphasize Five Essential Ingredients for a Local Church Peace Plan):

- **The plan is B*iblical* –** We have already established that the church is a divine institution; that it has a global redemptive mission, that the Holy Spirit is its Chief administrator or earth, and Jesus Christ the High Priest and Chief administrator in heaven. The chief opposition to the church is

Satan himself, the architect of conflict, violence and war (John 10:10A; Rev.12:7-13). It makes sense therefore, that a strategy to manage and resolve conflict is anchored in biblical values. Note well, that secular organizations resolve conflict differently because they are driven by secular *values, secular process*, and they get *secular outcomes*. Authentic Christian values are rooted in the word of God. Our knowledge base is different, our conflict resolution process different, and our outcomes are most often different.

- **The plan is *Residential.*** Residential means that the peacemaking mechanism is based at the local church. Church conflict is an inside job; it should be settled inhouse, in the community of faith, among the people of God. Most business corporations, institutions and organizations of significance have an inhouse dispute resolution system. The church should do no less.

- **The plan is *educational* and practical.** This means, it is part of the educational ministry of the church. The church must take an active role combating the culture of violence in the society. Violent video games, violent TV shows and movies, bullying at school, the gun culture all predispose children to violence. There has to be a counterculture and the church has an active role. All age groups from preschool to adult should be impacted by the peacemaking, peacekeeping ministry. Everyone must learn how to manage and resolve conflict peacefully, biblically. The ministry should be reflected in the church budget.

- **The plan is *lay leadership driven.*** Peacemaking and peacekeeping are the duties of every Christian. It is the business of every member of the church.

The Resident Counsel is the inhouse security force, the rapid response team. It formally manages and brings to resolution conflicted situations so that the unity of the church is not fractured or derailed from its mission, that the integrity of worship is maintained, and the message to the community and the world is not compromised. This approach keeps the pastor out of the heart of conflict, but it does not mean he or she is indifferent or mindlessly detached from what's happening.

- **The plan has *pastoral oversight*.** The pastor is involved in getting the ministry off the ground and off training-wheels. At this point he/she hands off the day to day function to trained lay leaders and step back. The pastor will provide help with continued training as part of ministry of the pastoral office (Eph.4:11-14). It is not in the congregation's interest or the pastor's to be in the heart of conflict (Acts 6:1-7). It will bring him/her to burnout and shortened pastoral tenure in short order.

- Review why the author prefers a lay leaders' conflict management system (CMS) over a Pastor-led conflict management system (CMS).

Lesson Application

Since conflict is inevitable and destructive conflict is preventable, a peace ministry at your church is a must and more so, if the church is going to live biblically and obediently to Christ. The peace ministry is one of the most effective ways to live out our Christian duties of peacemaking and peacekeeping.

A fire extinguisher is best placed at the location with the greatest potential for a fire. Conflict is like fire, the peace ministry is the extinguisher and the members the fire-preventers and fire-fighters, so an active inhouse peace ministry makes the most sense.

Furthermore, the onsite peace ministry gives the greatest opportunity to educate all members in their peacemaking and peacekeeping Christian duties, because they can put it in practice right there.

Finally, a residential peace ministry is best way to manage and resolve conflict doxologically (i.e. to the glory of God). The *Resident Counsel* of lay leaders run the ministry, all members take part, and the pastor helps with training and provides oversight.

LESSON 7

A BIBLICAL PRECEDENCE (OT)

Reading Assignment: (Read Textbook CH.6 and Review CH.5)

Lesson Purpose

In lesson 6, the preferred approach to conflict management and resolution at the local church is a lay leadership driven plan. Such peacemaking, peacekeeping plan has five essential ingredients or elements. Lesson 7 addresses the question of biblical precedence. Did this lay leadership approach recently fell out of the skies, or there is evidence for it among the people of God from the earliest of times?

The research concludes that—since God is consistent in His nature and character, if there is a preferred way He wants disputes settled among His people, there will be evidence of it in His spoken and written revelation. We should be able to draw insights from the start in the Old Testament.

Lesson Contents:

Precedence of God's preferred way of dealing with Conflicts (OT). Note well, the OT reveals that God wants conflict settled in the context of *justice restrained by mercy.* Bear this truth in mind during this discussion of what God wants. **Discuss the following:**

- **The concept of Precedence** as we know it in Western jurisprudence **VS** the *Law of First Mention* in the Bible. A position is not always stated in the law of first mention; it could be implied (e.g. justice and mercy, see next bullet).

- **How did God Himself first settle conflict**? Did He settle it in the context of justice restrained by mercy? Where is it first observed (law of first mention) in the Bible? (Answer: note the judicial proceeding with Adam and Eve after the fall. How did God show mercy here? First, he shows that fallen humans deserve redemption. Second, God driving them out of the garden was an act of mercy, less they eat from the Tree of Life and live forever in their sinful state (Gen.3:22-24). Next, note the judicial proceeding of God with Cain who violently ended his brother's life. Do you see justice and mercy here?

- After the Great Flood, *God protected the sanctity human life by authorizing capital punishing*. The person who murders another forfeits his own life. The message is, settle conflict peacefully because your life is at risk if you try Cain's solution to conflict.

Is there a lay-leaders precedence? Yes! It was first introduced by Jethro to Moses (Exod. 18:13-27).

- Moses was practicing the Pastor-led approach to dispute resolution with his congregation. His father-in-law enlightened him that his singular approach was not too smart; he should delegate some of that responsibility to lay people in his congregation. Moses accepted this wise counsel and adopted Jethro's delegated model. God later made it the official approach (Deut.1:5-15).

Institutional Precedence to Biblical Conflict Resolution

- Thanks to Jethro, dispute resolution was institutionalized under the giving of the Law. God put in writing His preferred way of conflict settlement. God wanted due process to protect the innocent and punish the guilty. The Priesthood was established as an institution of justice in part. Cities of Refuge protected the innocent from vigilante justice.

- God required justice and mercy in the Institutions of prophet and the King. The prophet speaks out against injustice and holds the king accountable (e.g. Samuel and Saul, David and Nathan, Elijah with Ahab and Jezebel. Micah (6:8) sums up what God wants.

Lesson Application

The OT has overwhelming evidence that God wants conflict settled in the context of justice restrained by mercy (Micah 6:8). It also shows that as early as the Exodus (18), God began using lay leaders to settle disputes among His people. Moses was a type of the senior pastor leading a congregation and singularly trying to settle all disputes among them. Jethro pointed out this approach to be inefficient and unhealth for both pastor and congregation; Moses agreed, God agreed and adopted Jethro's approach. Why was Moses' singular approach unhealthy?

- Because it puts the pastor in the hearth of conflict.
- Because it is inefficient; it squanders the valuable time of leader and people.
- Because it leads to pastoral overload and precipitates burnout.
- Because it prevents members exercising their ministry gifts.

Jethro provides the revelation of *delegated dispute resolution* that was hidden from Moses. He helped Moses to understand that the weight of such responsibility was too heavy for one person, that there are gifted lay people in his congregation that he could task to resolve disputes and take that weight of him. It will take wisdom and humility for a pastor not to think of himself or herself as superman or superwoman. Conflict by its very nature is energy depleting.

Instructors Notes

_____
_____
_____
_____
_____
_____
_____
_____
_____
_____
_____
_____
_____
_____
_____
_____
_____
_____
_____
_____
_____
_____
_____

LESSON 8

A BIBLICAL PRECEDENCE (NT)

Assigned Reading: (Read Textbook CH.7 and Review CH.6)

Lesson Purpose

Lesson 8 looks for God's preferred way for settling conflict among his people under the New Covenant. The focus here is on Jesus, the apostles and the early church. Did Jesus espouse a preferred way of managing and resolving conflicts? And did the apostles and the early church adopt and practice that preferred way? This lesson seeks to answer these questions and more.

Lesson Content

Precedence under the New Covenant—what are we looking for? Bear in mind that God's preferred way of settling conflict is in the context of *justice restrained by mercy*, as seen under the Old Covenant. Does this relationship between justice and mercy continues under the New Covenant? Also bear in mind that hidden in mercy is the concept of love which flows from a generous heart. **Have your students contemplate the following issues:**

- **Jesus fulfilled and revised the Law of Moses, the Torah (Genesis to Deuteronomy).** The entire Hebrew Bible (the Law, the Prophets, the Writings), what Christians call the OT, revolves around the Torah. Did

Jesus abolish the Law? No! He perfectly fulfilled it (Matt.5: 17-20). He also revised it; this revision is clearly seen in the Sermon on the Mount (Matt.5-7). Note the words, "It was said but I say." Jesus sums up the OT (Matt.22:34-40).

- **The New Covenant (Messianic) is personified in Jesus Christ Himself.** If you take Jesus Christ away, you have nothing left. He is the new law, the law of love. He redefines neighbor to include all our fellow human beings, even our enemies (Matt.5: 43-48). Christ is the new sacrifice, the new high priest, your body the new temple (the book of Hebrews explains all this).

- **Jesus peace theology is based upon His new law of love for God and neighbor which includes mercy.** "God is rich in mercy" (Eph.2:4). The practice of love is also the practice of mercy; you cannot have one without the other. Though God required love and mercy under the Old Covenant, the people of God woefully fell short of its practice (Micah 6:8). The Scribes and Pharisee greatly lacked mercy in the practice of their faith. Jesus said, "Blessed are the merciful for they shall obtain mercy" (Mat.5:7). The story of the Good Samaritan demonstrates a religion without the practice of mercy. Where mercy is short, love is also short, so conflict, violence and war rule.

- **Jesus became the new standard of righteousness**. It requires us to love God and neighbor, broadly defined. He orders us to put away the instrument of violence (the sword), turn the other cheek, go the extra mile, feed your enemy, do good to them that hate you. Jesus represents all this and more. The irony is, the Prince of peace died a violent death making peace (Rom.5:1-5; Eph.2:14-18). He prayed for the forgiveness of those who were murdering Him (Luke 23:34).

- ***Jesus' command to Peter to put away the sword, is a command to the whole church just as the gift of the keys to Peter is the gift of His authority to the church*** (Matt.26:51-54; John 18:10-**11**; Matt.16:17-19**).** The exercise of the authority of the sword is given to the State (the military and law enforcement). The State is a divine institution with the power of the sword (Rom.13:1-7). God also expects the State to render justice restrained by mercy to reflect His character. The church is given the authority the keys of the kingdom, not the sword (Matt.16:13-19).

The Apostles and the Early Church

The apostles and the early church provide clear and convincing evidence that they practiced the peace theology of Jesus in the management and resolution of conflict. **Discuss the following examples of precedence in resolving conflicts:**

- The church was birthed in the book of Acts (chapters 1 and 2). Were the followers of Christ persecuted by the authorities (the same actors that wanted Him dead)? Did the church fight back with the sword? No! Christians were not a sword wielding, anti-establishment, Barabbas-type revolutionary group; They were a nonviolent movement, peaceful and law abiding, persecuted and even murdered for their faith in Jesus Christ (Acts 3, 4,5,7, 8,9).

- ***How did they resolve conflict internally?*** By force from the top down? No! They used, democratic consensus. That's where lay-leaders were chosen to manage and resolve conflicts in the early church (Acts 6:1-7). A complaint of unfairness, ethnic discrimination, favoritism, nepotism was filed concerning the distribution of the temporalities of the church. Two groups in conflict, who were they, how did they settle this conflict? What kind of system did they put in place? What role did the apostles play? Is there a precedence here?

- *The second potential destructive conflict on record for the early Church—* concerns whether the church members, including gentiles, should be forced to conform to Jewish dietary laws and the ritual of circumcision to be saved (Acts 15:1-5). *When the local church could not resolve this conflict, what did **they do**?* **Answer:** they referred the case to a church arbitration (Acts 15:6-29). The arbitration happened to be a church council at the headquarters church in Jerusalem. Did the local churches abide by the arbitration ruling? **Answer:** Yes, gladly (Acts 15:30-35). Is there a precedence here?

- *A third conflict of interest is the one with Paul and Barnabas* **(Acts 15:36-41).** This dispute was over the young man named John Mark. He was a cousin of Barnabas. In a previous ministry assignment, Mark deserted the team and returned home (Acts 13:13). Perhaps, Paul fell he was unreliable and did not want him as part of the ministry team next time, but Barnabas wanted him. Paul would not compromise, and Barnabas would not compromise, and so they parted company. Barnabas taking Mark and Paul taking Silas (vv.39-41). **Point of emphasis**, *conflict can divide any church or ministry and separate chief friends.*

Lesson Summary and Application

First, God is not just mighty; He is Almighty, holy, righteous and just. He could really hurt His fragile human creatures, but His administration of justice is restrained by mercy. Furthermore, God wants His character of justice and mercy reflected in all human relationships: neighbor to neighbor, in families, in church and in the secular State administration of justice. God's justice and mercy are reflected in His dealings with human beings throughout the whole Bible, from Genesis to Revelation.

Second, among the people of God, we see ordinary lay leaders tasked to manage and resolve situations of conflict from the time of Moses to the apostles (Exod.18; Acts 6:1-7; Acts 15). Jesus came and set a higher standard for peaceful human relationships, one of nonviolence. Jesus took away the sword from the church and gave it to the ministers of the secular State (Rom.13:1-7). Here, God wants to see justice and mercy as well in the administration of justice among all peoples.

Third, we see precedence with the apostles and the early Church. The early church practiced the peace theology of Jesus. They used lay leaders to resolve situations of conflict in the church (Acts 6:1-7). In acts 15 we see lay leaders and apostles at an arbitration, working to manage and resolve a major conflict that a local church by itself could not resolve. **Point of emphasis**, the local church needs a conflict management system and connection to an arbitration body of believers. There is biblical precedence for both. *Students need to read chapter7 in the textbook to prepare for lesson 9.*

LESSON 9

A Historical Precedence

(Patristic to Reformation)

Word to the Instructor

This lesson covers *brief highlights* over an extensive period of history; it is easy to get bogged down or carried away into the vast wilderness of history. That is not the intent of this lesson. The textbook gives examples of several church councils that were convened to resolve conflicts, from Nicaea in 325 to Vatican II (that is Vatican 2). Vatican II was announced January 25, 1959 by Pope John XXIII and convened from 1962 to 1965.

These councils have been used as precedence to settle conflicts in the church and are still used by the Roman Catholic Church. In the Protestant camps, they are called by various names (Synods, Biannual meetings, Conventions, General Assembly, Convocation) and they have assigned a broader scope of fellowship and business at the denominational level.

The point is, councils great and small, have been convened throughout the history of the church to deal with conflict from its early beginning (Acts (6:1-7, 15:1-5). But somehow, many local churches got left behind without a conflict resolution system.

(Watch the movie *Luther* with your students or assign it. Here is the link (copy and paste the link in your computer browser). Or, go to Youtube and pullup: Luther, the movie. Compare that link with the link below, to ensure you have the right one. https://www.youtube.com/watch?v=_rJwCqhTyY8

Reading Assignment: (Read textbook CH.8 and Review CH.7)

Lesson Purpose

Lesson 9 seeks to understand how the church dealt with conflict during two tumultuous periods, from the church Fathers to the Reformation. The literature reveals that there were capable men referred to as *Church Fathers* who championed the cause of Christ even before the last apostle went off the scene; they fought for the faith which was once delivered unto the saints. They debated each other and convened councils where issues were further debated, and consensus reached on doctrinal matters.

This lesson asserts that the Church Fathers provide us with precedence as to how church conflicts were settled in the church and by the church. Students need to read chapter 7 in the textbook to get a better understanding of the subject and prepare for this lesson.

Lesson Content

- Define the Patristic period. The apostolic period came to an end at the closed of the first century (100 AD) when the last apostle died (the apostle John). The patristic period began about the ending of first century and runs to about 450 AD. The period is not neatly defined by scholars.

- The church suffered under State sponsored persecution but remains true to the nonviolent peace theology of Jesus toward conflicts within and from outside of the church. Conflicts from outside were political. Conflicts within were predominately doctrinal and were largely settled through church councils. Apart from the Jerusalem Council in Acts 15, the Council of Nicaea (325 AD) was the first major church council of its kind. It was convened by emperor Constantine.

- Emphasize when and how the church departed from the peace theology of Jesus and began to use the sword to settle conflict. Remember, Jesus did not give the sword to the church; He gave the keys instead (Matt.16:18-19). He gave the sword to the secular State (Rom.13:1-5). So, when did the church become violent? The short answer is—the church picked up the sword during medieval Papal Rome (that is after secular Rome fell). Papal Rome gave us the crusades and the inquisitions. The Augustinian Just War/Holy War theory was deployed and took on a life of its own, a brutal one; this brutality to saints and sinners, partly precipitated the Reformation.

- **Discuss the question:** Did the Protestant Reformation recapture the peace theology of Christ, or the Protestant arm of the church was nearly as violent as medieval Papal Catholicism?

Lesson Application

From the Jerusalem Council (Acts 15) to Vatican 2 and beyond, church councils have been used to resolve major doctrinal conflicts in the church. Roman Catholics and some major denominations even have church courts. This lesson, however, is not primarily about doctrine, but more about everyday relational issues that turn church members against each other and against their leaders to the point of doing serious damage.

In-as-much as the modern, postmodern and contemporary church no longer wield the sword as its medieval counterpart once did, she has not fully returned to the peace theology of Jesus Christ. If we did, a culture of conflict would not be woefully paralyzing many local churches. Yet, we have come a long way from the violent medieval church. Nonetheless, the people of God are called to be peacemakers; peace has to be intentionally pursued at the local church. But the pastor alone cannot do it; peacemaking and peacekeeping are the Christian duties of each member. That is why a lay leadership conflict management and resolution peace ministry is strongly advocated by this study.

Lay leaders managing and resolving conflicts have both Old and New Testament precedence, as well as precedence in the history of the church. It is one sure way the local church can reduce the culture of conflict, preserve the unity of the church, and safeguard the integrity of its message to the community and the world.

LESSON 10

UNDERSTANDING THE NATURE OF CONFLICT

Reading Assignment: (Read Textbook CH.9 and Review CH.8)

Lesson Purpose:

By now we should all understand what conflict is, normal conflict and destructive conflict. But taking a closer look at the nature of this animal will, perhaps, give us another or a clearer perspective. A simple dictionary definition will not do, but word pictures, symbols and metaphors can paint a better picture to aid our understanding of this human and animal behavior.

Jesus in His teaching about the kingdom of God, used symbols that were familiar to His audience. To fishermen, the kingdom is like a net thrown into the sea; to merchants, it is like a treasure buried in a field, and to farmers, it is like a sower sowing seeds. Jesus used stories or parables loaded with descriptive symbols of significance. In this lesson three symbols are used use to illustrate the nature of conflict: fire, hurricane, and cancer.

Destructive conflict is like fire (symbol #1)

Like fire, conflict is a good servant but a bad master. Conflict can help an organization to grow by stirring vigorous debate, bring new ideas to the table, thus preventing everybody from being a yes person, blindly following a strong or weak leader straight off the cliff. **Discuss how conflict is like fire:**

- Like fire, conflict has levels of destructive intensity. The intensity of a fire is expressed in alarms (3, 4, 5 alarms, etc.). The intensity of conflict moves from one level to another, up to five. But went a conflict no longer serves the general good, we often refer to it as destructive.

- Like fire, destructive conflict is preventable and controllable, if you prepare for it. But no matter how well you prepare, now and then, a conflict will cross the border from normal to destructive, and more so, if there is no system in place to manage and resolve it. A fire extinguisher at hand may prevent a small fire from burning you out of house and home.

- Like fire, conflict can be isolated, controlled or managed and extinguished (resolved). The discipline for resolving conflict is called, conflict management and resolution or dispute resolution or just peacemaking.

- Life fire, conflict not properly resolved can have hidden, smoldering ambers that can ignite a secondary fire in the same location. **Discuss** this concept of *smoldering ambers*.

So then, when conflict is viewed using the symbol of fire, we are saying it can serve your church or family well, but if it gets out of control, it can destroy everything in its wake. Normal conflict is inevitable and necessary; destructive conflict is *unnecessary*, *preventable*, *manageable* and *resolvable*. But you need a system in place; you need people with conflict management and resolution skills to do the hard work, not leaving it to chance. Where there is no peace ministry, conflict becomes destructive.

Destructive Conflict is like a Hurricane (symbol #2)

Most storms start at some distance away, in many cases as a tropical depression but they fizzle out quickly doing no harm, so we never heard of them. The winds cleanse the atmosphere and the water is harnessed for local use. But now and then, one of these systems develops intensity to become a hurricane. The higher the category, the greater threat it poses to life and property. Conflict is like hurricane in the following manner:

- like hurricane, conflicts can be destructive.
- like hurricane, conflict has five levels of intensity.
- like hurricane, conflict is almost unpredictable.
- like hurricane, conflict is costly to an organization.

A hurricane is as destructive as fire, both have the potential to destroy, but they are very different. You cannot control or manage a hurricane, but it gives you enough time to get out of its destructive path. Many churches have been given the storm-warning for years; they are told the big one is coming, prepare yourselves. Wisdom demands that you have a system in place; have a team of first responders. But some churches still have no peace ministry in place; they are left vulnerable and that includes leadership. Where is your church and its leaders stand, are ready for the big one?

Jesus forewarned His disciples about the coming storm of His death, but not one of them took Him seriously. They saw Him in many difficult positions before and He cleverly maneuvered Himself out of them. They refused to believe that the big one was coming. Every church and pastor need to prepare for destructive conflict that can undo them and everything they have worked for over the years. Don't be carried away with the cheers of Palm Sunday, betrayal, arrest, abandonment and crucifixion are coming, but they will be of your own negligence, not having a system to prevent them.

Destructive Conflict is like a Cancer (symbol #3)

- Cancer has four stages; conflict has five.
- Both have potential to destroy (reputation, career, life etc.)
- Both are costly (in money and human capital).
- You must manage and resolve it (medicine, surgery).

Lesson Summary and Application

If we summarized the three symbols of this lesson into one word that best reflect what the local church's attitude should be—the word would be "preparedness." Fire and gas constitute a lethal combination, but we combine them to cook each day without second thought. Yet, most kitchens don't even have a fire extinguisher to put out a small fire. We ignite (ignition) our car several times a day sitting on several gallons of gasoline with great explosive power, but how many of us have a fire extinguisher in our automobile? We hardly think about that, but it would not be paranoid to have one at hand; it may prove useful.

Cancer and hurricane require a different quality of preparedness to fire. Churches are more prone to conflict than kitchens and automobile to fire, but most churches are not prepared to deal with destructive conflict. But we can change this dynamic by intentionally becoming *agents of peace and managers* of conflict with this study. A new ministry of significance can be birthed at your church with this study. It is a peace ministry to help believers in their spiritual formation to be peacemakers and peacekeepers. Church folks can be taught the discipline that no matter what happen, never trash your church and disgrace your Lord.

SECTION III

UNDERSTANDING THE MECHANICS OF CONFLICT SETTLEMENT

(Lessons 11 to 15)

SECTION III: OVERVIEW

In this section, destructive conflict is viewed as you would an automotive malfunction or breakdown. To fix it, you must first diagnose the problem and you must have the appropriate tools and the knowledge to use the tools appropriately.

If we use a medical metaphor, the malfunction is in the human body. But in both cases, automobile or human body, you need a fixer, mechanic or surgeon with specialized training and tools. The fixer must also adhere to best practices to bring about a satisfactory outcome. The same is true in the resolution of conflict. In the context of destructive conflict, the problem is in human relationships; that calls for a unique body of knowledge, skills and tools to do the fix.

Five lessons are covered in this section. One is devoted to *causes and sources* of conflict and four to fixing the problem. The tools are drawn from two sources, the social sciences and the Bible, the Word of God. Why two sources? The social sciences have a secular worldview with its own set of values that produces a desired outcome. For this reason, secular conflict settlement has its own set of tools, herein called, general tools (Part 1 and 2).

The Biblical conflict settlement has its own unique worldview in which Christian beliefs, values and practices are anchored. For these reasons among others, the *process and outcomes* of Christian practice are uniquely Christian and different from its secular counterpart. Both bodies of knowledge are useful to each other in a limited way.

Process is how the *Agent of Peace* practitioner works the problem to achieve the desired fix or outcome. The biblical Christian process is different, and the outcome is often different as well.

Instructor's Notes:

_____

_____

_____

_____

_____

_____

_____

_____

_____

_____

_____

_____

_____

_____

_____

_____

_____

_____

_____

LESSON 11

CAUSES AND SOURCES OF CONFLICTS

Word to the Instructor

This lesson covers a significant amount of materials. Both instructor and students need to carefully do the assigned reading before class in order to extract the full benefit. There are two or more alternate ways to teach this lesson: devote one full session to major causes and another to minor causes or assign one or two causes per student to give a three to five-minute class presentation on (the alternative is optional is of course).

Reading Assignment: (Read Textbook CH.10 and Review CH.9)

Lesson Purpose:

The *causes and sources* of church and family conflicts are too numerous to catalog. Just about anything can develop into a destructive conflict. The personality of an individual, body language, choice of words and tone of voice can add fuel to the fire. People often say, "It is not what you said; it is how you said it." The ability to navigate difficult communications is critical to defusing conflict.

Sometimes people feel insulted, disrespected, embarrassed and those feelings can escalate the fight or become the fight. Indeed, "Soft answer turns away wrath, but a harsh word stirs up anger" (Prov.15:1 NKJV). This lesson looks at some common sources and causes of organizational conflict, especially churches. The terms *major* and *minor* do not mean one is more or less important than the other but to show that conflict, like a forest fire, can start from an insignificant spark.

Major Causes and Sources of Conflict (Briefly explore these nine sources and causes).

1. People fight over *values* and *beliefs*. Beliefs are our world views, rooted in tradition and history. Values are our preferred ways of doing things; they are rooted in our belief system. Some values are deeper than others, so they are vested with more emotions or passion.

2. Unclear church structure (i.e. organizational structure).

3. Pastor's role and responsibilities (Pastor doing too little or too much or overstepping his or her role thus confusing other leaders).

4. Outgrown governance structures (include archaic buildings)

5. Pastoral leadership style Versus Church Tradition

6. Untimely or abrupt change implementation

7. Ineffective channels of communication

8. Retaliation of dissatisfied members

9. Untrained church members. Church folks are generally not trained to deal with conflict. For this reason, they are the ones that destroy their own church, not the unbelievers on the outside.

Minor Causes and Sources of Conflict (Briefly discuss these nine sources and causes)

1. Wrongful or unfair treatment (experienced by leadership or member)
2. Feelings of being dominated by superior (experienced by member)
3. Suspension of privilege or perceived entitlement (experienced by leader or member).
4. Undiagnosed mental health problem (in member or leader)
5. Dictatorial leadership and insubordinate followers
6. Church members unable to exercise their gifts
7. Unrecognized service (experienced by leader or member)
8. Leadership compensation
9. Leadership visibility (Pastor is often gone)

Summary and Application:

In this lesson, we have briefly covered eighteen causes and sources of conflict in the church; a few of them overlap of course. There is much more to be said on theses headings at the intermediate and advanced levels of training. Furthermore, this is not an exhaustive list, and the headings are not set in concrete, other people may frame them differently.

In other words, some of these causes and sources of conflict can manifest themselves in various ways in different churches and peoples, so the list may not fit in every setting exactly the same way. As you observe disagreements in your church overtime, you may well be able add *causes and sources* that are not listed here. These are common and frequent but not necessarily exhaustive.

The preceding is true because conflict can start over just about anything, especially where people are short on the practice of love. Love is kind, patient and does not keep a list of wrongs done, in order to respond with unkindness when opportunity avail itself (1Cor.13). Love indeed covers a multitude of faults and can deal with differences in people. Someone defines conflict as "power struggle over differences."

Instructor's Notes:

_____
_____
_____
_____
_____
_____
_____
_____
_____
_____
_____
_____
_____
_____
_____
_____
_____
_____
_____
_____
_____

LESSON 12

GENERAL PEACEMAKING TOOLS - PART 1

Word to the Instructor

This lesson covers core materials. Instructor and students need to carefully do the assigned reading (chapter 10) before class. There are ten (10) general peacemaking tools and they are covered in two lessons (12 and 13). Five of the ten tools or principles are deal with in this lesson. Student will get an introductory understanding of how each works in both secular and Christian dispute resolution.

Reading Assignment: (Review Textbook CH.10)

Lesson Purpose

When we speak of peacemaking tools, we are referring to the concepts or principles used by practitioners to manage and bring conflicted situations to resolution. The general principles are called general because they are largely drawn from the social sciences and are used by both secular and Christian practitioners but in markedly different ways.

The general principles form an *indispensable knowledge base* for all dispute resolution practitioners, but these principles cannot stand alone for the Christian practitioner. Why? Because Christian peacemaking is driven by a *different set of values*. For this reason, the *peacemaking process* is also different. Process is how you get from point-A to point-Z. If the process is different, the outcome will most likely be different as well in many cases. As each principle is discussed, the student should be asking, how is the Christian process different?

Lesson Contents

The Principles of Prevention:

- **First**, bear in mind that you, as an *Agent of Peace-Manager of Conflict*, are not trying to prevent conflict entering your church or organization. Conflict is inevitable where people of free will come together. Conflict is good for an organization. It allows for the free exchange of ideas, different perspectives and vigorous debates, which are all good for growth and development of the organization.

- **Second**, you the agent of peace tries to prevent conflict from becoming destructive. So then, there is normal conflict and abnormal or destructive conflict. Conflict becomes destructive when people turn upon each other and when the conflict no longer serves the general good or interests of the organization.

- **Third,** how do you prevent conflict from becoming destructive? In the church, it is everybody's business to work for peace because it is a Christian duty. But we should not assume that every member knows that. So, the church needs a peace ministry to take on the task of educating the members and serve as an inhouse team to resolve situations of conflict. In other words, conflict has to be managed to prevent it from becoming destructive. If and when it becomes destructive, the system in place continues to manage it to bring it to resolution before it paralyzes the entire church.

- **Fourth,** note the role of the Agent of peace-Manager of Conflict: Provider, Teacher, Bridge-builder. The *provider* helps to meet the needs of the person that gives rise to conflict. The teacher educates, so people acquire knowledge to meet their own needs. The *bridge-builder* builds relationships, perhaps between haves and the have nots.
- **Fifth,** overlook a matter: some things are insignificant and not worth fighting over. This will be discussed later, but worth putting on the table early as a conflict prevention strategy.

The Principle of Avoidance

Avoidance can be both a positive and a negative principle in the resolution of conflict. Humans and animals in the face of danger prepare for *fight* or *flight*. This is a normal biological response to threat or danger. In a church setting, some members will stay home or flee to cross-town church, while others will dig their heels in and fight the powers that be.

Avoidance can also trigger a wide range of defense mechanisms in the face of conflict: denial, rationalization, suppression, even suicide, to name a few. Individuals under serious scandal and disgrace can turn on themselves as the law begins to close in on them. Some resign rather than fight, others commit suicide.

Both the secular and the Christian peacemakers are faced with the principle of avoidance but the values that drive Christian practice are often different. For that and other reasons, Christians are not quick to commit suicide or murder in a crisis or conflict. But why? It is because we are so good and well self-controlled? Not really! The answer is much deeper than that.

Yes, we are more restrained because we are spiritually enlightened and restrained by the word of God, the Holy Spirit, our Christian brothers and sisters, and even the angels of God that camp around us and minister to us (Ps.34:7; Heb.1:14). But we will hate, and the Bible calls that murder (Matt.5:21-261; John 3:15). We are responsible for guarding our own heart.

Some members flee to cross-town church rather than face the problem of conflict and deal with it. This form of escapism is not healthy. Often, people keep running until they drop out of church altogether or they face the problem, repent, get renewed and restored. In most cases, the problem lies within them.

The Principle of Negotiation

Negotiation or bargaining is a core principle widely used in peacemaking and deal-making; it is used in all forms of dispute resolution or conflict settlement in society, even in buying a product at the store. You haggle or bargain over the price; that is a form of negotiation.

Negotiation is used to secure different types of outcomes: win/lose, win/win or to secure a compromise. The authentic, biblical peacemaker uses it doxologically; that is to the glory of God. The supreme goal of Christian resolution is to settle conflict to the glory of God. When you are in a conflict, quietly ask yourself, how can I glorify God in this situation? What would Jesus do? How can I settle this to His honor and glory? Hidden in conflict is an opportunity to serve the others. In this case, the person that is disputing with you.

Another principle that is frequently deployed in negotiation is the interests of the other party, your opponent. So, shift the focus from what you want to what the other person wants. Even a hostage-taker needs something, so the FBI negotiator will ask, what does he want? This question speaks to the hostage-taker's interests.

Next, try to meet that interest or need in a win/win way; there is a good chance of getting the hostages back alive. For starters, the FBI may say, I will give you food and water, you release the women and children. Of course, the Christian negotiator has to meet a higher bar than a mere win/win, win/lose or lose/lose outcome. For the Christian, the outcome has to be *doxological*. Rather than fight, Abraham stepped back and put the interest of Lot first. In the short-term, it looks like Abraham got the worst of the deal, but the story shows differently.

The Principle of Mediation

The principle of mediation is often used when the two sides in a dispute are unable to come to a resolution of the problem, so they agree for a third party to help them work through the process. It's like wife and husband agreeing for a marriage therapist to help them work through their difficulties. Like negotiation, mediation is widely used in all forms of conflict settlement.

For the Christian, mediation is not new; it is a biblical principle. Christians in their salvation relationship with God has a mediator named, Jesus Christ (Rom.5:1-3; Eph.2). Note well that while negotiation is primarily focused on the interests of persons, mediation is more focused on the relationship between persons. The wife and husband want to resolve the dispute because they want to save their marriage. The marriage could be a business partnership. For the relationship to continue the problem has to be resolved.

Again, sometimes the problem does not worth the fight, so you overlook the problem for the sake of the relationship. We often use the colloquial term, let it slide. Of a course, if a person is taking a dollar-a-day from the petty cash, it will add up to three hundred and sixty-five dollars ($365) at year's end and has to be accounted for. So, there are some small things, if they keep recurring, cannot be overlooked; you have to be dealt with.

The Principle of Accommodation

To accommodate is to go along with your opponent because it is the advantageous thing to do in the short-term or in the long-term. Accommodation is an everyday principle used by ordinary people in all walks of life. But specialists also use it to avoid or resolve conflicted situations. In accommodation, you sit-down with the other side and work out the problem. They bring ideas to the table; you bring ideas to the table.

Some practitioners view accommodation as part of the principle of negotiation. For example, a restaurant owner agrees to the ridiculous salary demands of his chief cook, because losing him is detrimental to his restaurant business. The cook makes the restaurant. Or, the FBI negotiator agrees to the demands of the hostage taker for the sake of the lives of the hostages.

The biblical principle of turning the other cheek and going the extra mile is a form of accommodation. The mother who offered up her baby rather than having him cut in halves in a Solomon's compromise was using the principle of accommodation, though not known to her at the time. If someone is making a big fuss over a minor thing you say, okay, okay! I will go along with that. You have just accommodated the person.

Summary and Application

The five dispute resolution tools (principles) covered in this lesson belong to a group of ten; the other five are covered in lesson 13. That is how this author views these working principles; they are like levers used to accomplish something else.

The principle of avoidance is hardly a formal tool; practitioners don't say, well we are going to use the avoidance method to resolve this problem. But the leaders of an organization will meet to discuss how they can avoid litigating this dispute in court. It will cost them more, and the press will get a hold of it and that's not good for business. So, it is in the best interest of the organization to settle the matter.

On the other hand, we see avoidance as a biological response to conflict. Conflict is painful and costly, so we seek to avoid it by flight or fight.

But we also see that avoidance can trigger a wide range of defense mechanism in response to conflict such as denial, suppression, rationalization and so on. The more popular of the five principles are negotiation, mediation and accommodation which lead to prevention. You can prevent a conflict becoming destructive because there is a system in place to bring it to resolution.

LESSON 13

GENERAL PEACEMAKING TOOLS – PART 2

Reading Assignment (Read Textbook CH.10)

Lesson Purpose

This lesson is of the same purpose as lesson 12; it continues the discussion on general principles used in secular dispute resolution field which are also used by Christian practitioners, but in different ways. Christians have a different set of values based on a different belief system or worldview. These values are biblically rooted to inform and influence the conflict resolution process and most often the outcome as well.

In the Christian context, conflict with other human beings is settled doxologically. Secular dispute resolution does not intentionally make room for glorifying God in settling any conflicted business transactions. Theirs is generally a win/win or win/lose proposition.

As stated earlier, this lesson adds five more principles or tools to the five stated in the previous lesson thus making a total of ten general tools. A few of these principles are not stand-alone settlement tools; they are mostly used as supplementary tools. In fact, a dispute resolution session is hardly ever locked into a singular tool. That is why the practitioner should have several wrenches in his toolbox and be proficient with them all.

The Principle of Confrontation

The principle of confrontation is largely adversarial, but it is actually a negotiation strategy. It is often used by law enforcement and unions in collective bargaining. Sometimes in law enforcement, it serves as a balance between the good cop, bad cop approach.

Confrontation has its place in a wide range of conflict situations. A special prosecutor uses it to arrive at the truth. It is a form of persuasion which can be forceful or gentle. Issuing a subpoena is a persuasion tool to get an opponent's cooperation. Union bargains aggressively to secure the outcome they want, and they will even call a strike to secure a satisfactory outcome. All these tactics are confrontational in nature.

Confrontation, like all the other principles, should be viewed as one tool among many in a practitioner's toolkit to be deployed when needed. There are people with a confrontational personality, and they tend to use it at the sight of every conflict, and it never fails to get them in trouble.

The Principle of Leadership

Leadership is a universal principle because it is need in all approaches to dispute resolution. Wise leadership is particularly critical in organizational dispute resolution and peacemaking.

Leadership is a privilege that requires a certain temperament, competence, knowledge, wisdom and insight. Leadership also carries responsibility and accountability. Experienced leaders know how to use conflict appropriately to accomplish positive outcomes; they embrace conflict rather than avoid it. Experienced leaders can see new solutions and even opportunities in conflict and use it to their advantage. It is true, "where there is no vision, the people perish" (Prov.29:18 KJV).

The Principle of Collaboration

The core of collaborating is working with people you disagree with, but you have to for the greater good. This is a common core principle that is used in all forms of human relationships: in the family, work, church and in societal institutions.

A church is normally made up of different departments or auxiliaries with leaders. A department leader cannot dominate the calendar without regard for the overall organization; that will bring conflict with departments which is not good for the organization. Coordination and collaboration are always necessary for smooth operation. This mode of operation is true from small to large enterprises or organizations.

Some consider collaboration the ideal principle of dispute resolution without which a democratic society with majority rule would never work.

The Principle of Arbitration

Arbitration is an independent body that parties in a dispute agree to have their case referred for resolution and abide by its ruling. The approach is widely recognized in dispute resolution and its ruling is generally recognize by the courts.

The Jerusalem Counsel served as a form of arbitration for the early church (Acts 15). Local churches should ensure their church is connected to such body in case they reach an impasse on any issue. If there is no denominational entity to serve as arbitration; the pastors of local church or association may have to form their own.

The Principle of Litigation

The principle of litigation is when redress is sought through courts. The Bible is not anti-court. The courts are part of the secular state, a necessary institution ordained by God for an orderly society. God has given to the secular state the administration of justice (Rom.13:1-7).

Christians will need the court system, at one time or another. Western jurisprudence is largely based upon the Judea-Christian system of justice. So, the courts are not totally heathen as first century Palestine when Christianity was in its infancy. There are believers throughout the entire court system today, but even so, the church is charged with settling its own conflicts. The Lord requires believers to settle their disputes in the community of faith rather than in the public civil court (Matt.18:15-18; 1Cor.6:1-8).

Summary and Application

Between lessons 12 and 13, we have covered ten principles (5+5) usually used in secular dispute resolution but used by Christians as well, though differently. Most of these principles or tools are used as supplemental principles rather than standalone tools. Just as fixing a mechanical or surgical problem requires several tools, so is conflict management and resolution. The practitioner needs several tools in his or her toolkit.

For the Christian practitioner, these secular tools serve as a good knowledge base, but they cannot stand on their own when resolving conflict within an authentic Christian setting such as the church. Why? Christians live by a different set of values to unbelievers, values that are anchored within the word of God. Believes seek to do all to the glory of God.

LESSON 14

BIBLICAL PEACEMAKING TOOLS - PART 1

Reading Assignment: (Read Textbook CH.11)

Lesson Overview and Purpose

In the previous two lessons, ten general principles or tools used by both secular and Christian practitioners in dispute resolution, bargaining and peacemaking are discussed. For the Christian peacemaking practitioner, the ten general themes are inadequate on their own. They form a useful knowledge base but fall short of the required essentials for biblical peacemaking.

This lesson covers five of ten essential themes that must be merged with the general themes to bring about a dispute resolution process and outcome that is truly biblical and authentically Christian. The next lesson (15) will cover the remaining five themes.

Christians values are markedly different from the humanistic values that drive secular dispute resolution approaches. Christian peacemaking that is biblically anchored, seeks to conform to the peace theology of Jesus as set forth in the New Testament (NT). This lesson covers five of these themes: repentance, confession, forgiveness, reconciliation and restitution.

Lesson Contents for Discussion:

The Principle of Repentance

Repentance is not normally a required element in secular dispute resolution. It is a biblical word which means a change of mind, attitude, disposition and direction. It is a complete turn-around. The key word in repentance is change, change within the offender that is so profound, it causes him or her to think and behave differently; it even causes him to change direction.

Repentance, therefore, is almost always used in the context of one-party taking responsibility for the hurt, offence or damage he or she caused to another and now wants to remedy, to make amends. The offended party could be human or God. Repentance implies acts of contrition and remedy. **Discuss King David's offence** against Uriah and God and show what was done to remedy the matter.

Destructive conflict almost always involves offense, real or perceived, done by one person or group to another person or group of persons. This offense could be unfairness in some matter, injustice, violation of rights, loss or threatened loss of property. If satisfactory remedy is not brought to bear on the problem in a timely manner, schisms, violence and even war could erupt.

The Principle of Confession

Confession means the offender comes clean by taking responsibility for the offence, tell the full and complete truth. This action of confession is made to the offended party, man or God.

Note well, confession is inextricable tied to repentance; you cannot have one without the other. Discuss the following:

- Ken Sande's Seven A's to confession (TB CH.11).
- Why is confession good for the soul? (James 5:16).

The Principle of Forgiveness

Forgiveness is a bedrock principle in Christian dispute resolution that is now being used by some secular practitioners. Forgiveness is a broad topic with many turns and nuances to it. But fundamentally, it is a decision reached by the injured party not to take personal revenge or exact excessive and unjust actions against the offender now or ever, even to wish the offender's wellbeing.

It is important to note that forgiveness does not mean any of the following:

- It does not mean—the injured party is no longer hurting.
- It does not mean—the injured party has forgotten the injury that was inflected.
- It does not mean legal consequence will not follow; the District Attorney will pursue some cases whether victims want to or not.
- It does not mean—it is okay to keep stolen property or money embezzled.

Name and discuss the fourfold path to forgiveness used by Archbishop Desmond TuTu, in his work of forgiveness and as chairman of *The Truth and Reconciliation Commission,* bringing healing to post-apartheid South Africa when Nelson Mandla became President of that country.

"Just drop it" are my words for what Ken Sande calls, "Overlooking an Offence" (Sande 2004, 25). It is a biblical principle (Prov.19:11; Col.3:13) that practitioners consider important to include in dispute prevention discussion and application. The idea here is to overlook and let go of insignificant infractions or trespass before they fester and develop into major dispute. In other words, just drop it! It is the spark, if allowed, could develop into a regrettable firestorm.

The Principle of Restitution

Restitution is the return of property wrongfully taken from its owner. Sometimes it takes the form of compensation for damages done to a person's good name or reputation. Slander, liable, doing damage to one's name or reputation is very serious and compensation damage is very much in order. Some believers tend to gloss over this matter, not take it seriously. To God and civil law it is a serious matter.

On the one hand, restitution is separate from forgiveness, yet linked to *forgiveness* and *repentance,* on the other hand. Using the story of Zacchaeus, discuss this dual link and its implication for Christian conduct (Luke19:18).

Class exercise—Jane, a mother of two school age children, was financial secretary for First Baptist Church. It was her paid job to count the weekly contributions, deposit it in the bank, and handed the record to the treasurer. It's a job she took on since her pastor husband died suddenly and she had to move out of the parsonage to make way for the new pastor. It was discovered that overtime, Jane had embezzled $75,000 of the church's money.

You are sitting on the Board of Trustee and must vote to have her arrested and serve time in the County prison, what alternative action could you recommend to the board short of her going to prison? For example, one trustee recommends that she be fired from the job, payback the money and that she be disfellowshipped from the church. Come up with a plan and state your reason for such a plan.

Some have argued that forgiveness is the cancellation of a debt, therefore, once it is given there is no need for restitution. What is wrong with this understanding of forgiveness and restitution?

The Principle of Reconciliation

To reconcile is to bring persons into peaceful relationships. The principle of reconciliation is closely connected to the principle of forgiveness. Reconciliation has to do with the restoration of a fractured or broken relationship. It is the ideal end goal of biblical forgiveness. Forgiveness and reconciliation are at the heart of the gospel. Jesus died that we might be forgiven and be reconciled to God and each other (Rom.5:1-5; 2Cor.5:17-21).

Reconciliation is critical to acceptable worship, including fellowship at the Lord's Table (Matt.5:22-24; 1Cor.11:23-32). Secular dispute resolution, with the exception filial relationships, hardly speaks of reconciliation. Instead they speak of getting along, tolerance, and civility of interpersonal behavior which do not carry the gravitas of biblical reconciliation.

Discuss the question: Bearing in mind that the core meaning of reconciliation is the *restoration of relationship.* Is reconciliation always possible and if not, what do you do with the fractured or broken relationships?

Summary and Application

We have discussed five of the ten biblical principles or tools used in the resolution of conflict and peacemaking in the Christian context. You can clearly see that these five principles are fundamental Christian values, anchored in the word of God. These five values already show you how the process of Christian dispute resolution is markedly different from the approaches of the secular disciplines.

Repentance, confession, forgiveness, restitution and reconciliation are all related to one degree or another when addressing offence toward God and neighbor. A healthy relationship with God and neighbor warrants periodic review of these five relational themes. Genuine repentance toward God includes: the acknowledgement of sin (the wrong), confession of sin (coming clean with the truth) and turning away from the wrong. It includes a resolve not to repeat the wrong again. The same steps are necessary if I hurt or offend my neighbor.

Confession is good for the soul; it unburdens the soul of guilt. Forgiveness is a decision we make to bury that hatchet, not to carry a grudge against the offender. Restitution is the act of returning property taken wrongfully. Some things we take from people cannot be returned, so compensation might be in order. How do you restore a person's reputation and good name? How does a rapist give a young woman back her virginity? How does a murderer give back a grieving mother her son?

Reconciliation of relationship is the ideal thing to work for in forgiveness, but in some cases, you grant forgiveness, but reconciliation of the relationship is not possible. For example, rape, murder, and some form of domestic violence. What do you do? The victim makes the determination without coercion or religious, puritanical pontification as to what direction to go. In some cases, the relationship cannot be renewed. So, you release the relationship that both parties can go their separate ways and go on with life.

LESSON 15

BIBLICAL PEACEMAKING TOOLS - PART 2

Reading Assignment: (Read textbook Ch.12 and review Ch.11)

Lesson Purpose

This lesson is focused on five additional principles or tools Christians used in the resolution of conflict in faith communities. They are the interest of others, the love of God, accountability, discipline and restoration to fellowship.

Again, they are not all stand-alone tools; few of them are supplemental tools, used to support other principles. "The interest of others" is commonly used in general negotiation, bargain and deal making but its origin is biblical. For the Christian agent of peace-manager of conflict, these are value laden principles that are normally expected in the Christian life and in interaction with neighbors. We are called upon to *do justly* and to *love mercy* (Micah 6:8).

Lesson Contents

The Interest of Others

Discuss the origin of this concept in human relationship. The Christian faith is around for over two thousand years, so it predates by far the social sciences as we know them today. Yet, the apostle Paul exhorted the Philippians believers in the first century (A.D. 60-62) with these words, "Let nothing be done through selfish ambition or conceit, but in lowliness of mind let each esteem others better than himself. Let each of lookout not only for his own interests, but also for the interests of others" (Phil.2:3-4 NKJV).

It is also clear that Paul did not practice this principle in his native Hebrew religion. If he had, he would not have led a murderous campaign to destroy people who disagreed with him. It is clearly evident that the principle came from the teachings of Jesus, first seen in the Sermon on the Mount (Matt.5-7). It is here we first encounter the adjustment from the Law of Moses to the law of Christ, to love your enemy. Is there any better recipe to end human conflict, violence and war? It is now been clearly understood that if you want to get your own needs met, pay attention to the needs of others. In a conflict, find out what is the interest or need of your opponent and help him or her to achieve it, and you stand an excellent chance of resolving that conflict and build a sustainable relationship.

Christian dispute resolution is not based upon winners take all or upon a win/lose proposition or even on win/win outcome. Every follower of Christ knows that Jesus gave up all for our sakes (Phil.2:5-11). Sometimes for peace sake, we turn the other cheek, go the extra mile, even surrender our rights for others. No secular dispute orientation practice this, even though to some extent, they borrow the interest of others concept. But the farthest they will go is to allow for a win/win proposition.

Christ calls His disciples to a higher standard of righteousness, one that exceeds that of the Scribes and Pharisees (Matt.5:20). That standard is not diluted in our dispute resolution; that is one reason we say, "For the Christian, conflict must be settled doxologically."

The Love of God Principle

The love of God principle brings us back to the peace theology of Jesus, which is built upon the new command to love God and neighbor and the practice of justice restrained by mercy.

It is in this context, Jesus commands us to surrender the sword, the instrument of violence and work for peace. For this reason, the sword is not given to the church; it is given to the secular state for an orderly society (Rom.13:1-7). The church is given the authority and power of the keys of the kingdom to make peace and reconcile people to God and each other (Matt.16:16-18; 2Cor.5:17-21).

Emphasize to your students that love for God is inextricably bound to love for neighbor. You cannot love God and hate your neighbor; you are your brother's keeper (1John 3:11-18). How is it then that we fight at the local church, and without settling our conflict, we run off to cross-town church to take up membership there. Is it any wonder we have the same result as taking communion unworthily? We are weak and sickly and some die.

The greatest of all spiritual gift is the practice of love (1Cor.13; Gal.5:22). Wherever conflict rules, there is a shortage of true love in practice. We talk a good talk, but our walk has not caught up yet with our talk.

The Accountability Principle

In Christian conflict resolution and peacemaking, there is the principle of accountability. In the church of Jesus Christ everybody is accountable to somebody, that is how we come under the Lordship of Christ. The church is likened to the human body with many members under one head (1Cor.12:12-20). Leaders and members in the church are under the same headship of Christ (12:27; Eph. 4: 11-13).

Leaders are accountable to Christ, their congregations, and their governing boards. The congregation is accountable to Christ and their leaders (Heb.13:17). And so, we submit to each other as we submit to Christ. This reciprocal act of submitting to one another in the body of Christ is beautifully illustrated using the metaphor of marriage (Eph.5:21-33).

Because of pride and even arrogance, leaders don't want to submit to their congregation, and members behave in a similar way. Members would rather run off to crosstown church than submit. Some pastors would rather label their congregation difficult to lead and seek tenure somewhere else than submit to their congregations.

Frankly, many pastors do not even know that submitting to their congregation is a biblical concept (Eph.5:21). Beyond the professional pastoral role, the congregation constitutes a priesthood of believers under Christ (1Peter 2:5,9). The pastor is part of that priesthood of believers submitting to one another under the authority of Christ. So, there is a dual accountability here.

The Principle of Discipline
Discuss the concept of church discipline with your students. Is church discipline alive and well today, or dead and non-existent? How does your church exercise discipline, if any? Is there still a mourner's bench? Are members disallowed from taking Holy communion?

The very word disciple implies discipline. The Lord of the church exercises discipline over His people through His church (Heb.12:4-12). But if church members and leaders refuse to submit to each other in love like a marriage, that church will have great difficulty exercising and submitting to discipline. The governing board of a church should be strong enough to exercise discipline over all its leaders in love on behalf of the congregation (Matt.18:15-18).

On the other hand, the under-shepherd or pastor should have the spiritual and moral authority with the governing board to discipline any member of the congregation. Of course, the administration of discipline should not be the singular job of the pastor, but the collective will of the whole congregation. Discipline includes disfellowshipping a member, even handing him or her over to Satan (1Cor.5:1-5). Singular discipline has the risk of abuse.

Church discipline is both "formative and corrective," asserts Mark Denver. The one is preventative; it uses instruction in the word to shape a life toward godly living. The other is deployed when trouble arises. It includes "contradicting, challenging, rebuking, and excommunicating" (Denver in Holman Study Bible, article).

Why corrective discipline, particularly excommunication, should not be singularly carried out by the pastor? (Answer: It puts the pastor in the heart of conflict and one person should not singularly disfellowship a member). The authority to disfellowship a member is vested in the corporate body, not one individual. Such authority could be easily abused in the hands of one person.

The Principle of Restoration

Perhaps, the most severe aspect of church discipline is excommunication; the member is drop from fellowship and sometimes handed back to Satan. Some writers assert that excommunication and handing the member back to Satan are one and the same. Because the church has returned the member to the camp of the unbelievers which is Satan's domain. The member is returned there because he is behaving like an unbeliever. Be that as it may, there should be a plan to restore that person to faith and fellowship when the discipline has run its course, and there is evidence of repentance.

Why should there be a plan for restoration? The church is a family; as such, it should have care and compassion for those that have fallen. Not to have a well-coordinated plan to work with that member and restore him or her to fellowship is at best cruel and abusive.

A church cannot just discord a precious soul for whom Christ died and think it is okay; it is not! The apostle Paul gives us this intelligence, "Brethren, if a man be overtaken in a trespass, you who are spiritual restore such a one in a spirit of gentleness, considering yourself less you also be tempted. Bear one another's burdens, and so fulfill the law of Christ (Gal.6:1-2 NKJV).

In light of the Galatians passage (6:1-2), the person or persons assigned to do this ministry of restoration should not be a novice Christian because there is a risk of being dragged under. A novice swimmer should not be assigned the task of rescuing a drowning person. The work of restoration is gentle, not fraught with condemning and judgmental attitudes or platitudes. It should be done in love. The law of Christ is love. The restoration to fellowship is not only an act of love on the part of the church, it is the continued work of discipleship.

Discuss the restoration of Peter to apostleship after his denial of Jesus, (John 18:15-18,25-27; John 21:1-19). If time allows, discuss the restoration of the prodigal son to the family (Luke 15:13-32).

Lesson Summary and Application

Between lessons 14 and 15, we have looked at ten indispensable biblical principles or tools used in Christian conflict management and resolution. These ten principles are used to regulate another ten drawn from the secular discipline of conflict resolution, negotiation and peacemaking. The ten biblical principles of conflict settlement are among what make the Christian practice unique and distinctive. They represent beliefs and value that biblical and unapologetically Christian.

The five principles covered in lesson 15 brings us deeper into the peace theology of Jesus Christ. They capture the heart of Christ for His people. They show us how to love and care for each other, how to discipline in love, and how to restore the fallen to fellowship as Jesus did for Peter; this love is also demonstrated in the story of the Prodigal Son.

SECTION IV

ESTABLISHING A RESIDENT COUNSEL MINISTRY IN YOUR CHURCH

(Lessons 16 to 20)

SECTION IV

OVERVIEW

Section IV shows you how to launch a peace ministry at your local church. Invest all you have been taught about peacemaking and peacekeeping in establishing a peace ministry at your church. When you launch a peace ministry, you are mobilizing the entire congregation to become a peace-loving, peacemaking, and peacekeeping church or people. Peacemaking is the identity of the people of God (Matt.5:9).

First, you conduct conflict education training for the entire church. Second, you organize a lay team called, the *Resident Counsel* or whatever you wish to name it. The counsel is commissioned to do its work. Third, there is the work phase and continued training of the counsel. This includes identifying new members coming into the church and recruiting them for training. A house only needs one careless person to burn it down. Peacemaking is every member's Christian duty.

There are five lessons in this section: two address the critical issue of corporate unity including social media, and three address the practical aspects of training and implementation.

LESSON 16

PRESERVING CORPORATE UNITY

Reading Assignment: (John 17; Acts 2: 42-47; 4:12-35). Scripture focus the unity of the Body.

A Word to the Instructor

Throughout this study, reference is frequently made to the unity of the *Body of Christ* (the Church) but this lesson is singularly devoted to this critical issue of corporate unity or the unity of the local church. Like links in a chain, each member in a local church is a link in the *bond of unity* that binds the entire congregation together. In the Baptist Church it is often referred to as a covenant relationship. Your students need to know that without this understanding of unity, the other three lessons in this section is little more than an exercise in futility.

The other three lessons in this section talk directly to students who may one day become instructors themselves. They don't know it yet, but once they have taken this *Basic Training* course, chances are, they will want to teach the course in the future to other church groups and, perhaps, charge a fee for doing so. The course is a worthy investment.

Since the possibility of students becoming instructors exist, approach training with a broad vision, that students may afterword want to do the *Intermediate* and *Advanced Trainings* that will qualify them to teach the course. For this and other reasons, it makes sense for all students to learn the structure of the course; they may even come up with creative ways to improve its contents and structure.

Furthermore, ensure that you, the present planners and instructors, preserve accurate records of this *Basic Training* for future reference; this includes students' attendance records, scores on short quizzes, reading assignment, and scores on the final exam as well.

The three structural lessons following this, may appear easy but bear in mind that planning a training course has many moving parts that the planners have to think through months before the actual training commences. So, encourage students to give attention and creativity to the process; they may come up with new ideas that may serve them well.

Lesson Purpose

The purpose of this lesson is to help the student understand the nature of biblical unity in relation to the body of Christ, and why corporate unity is critical to the mission of the church.

Lesson Content

The unity of a church is much more than the presence of the physical bodies of members in a building. People can be members of the same church and they are neither in fellowship or unity; neither do they have any depth sense of loyalty to Christ or each other. The corporate quality of unity of which we speak is reflected in several New Testament (NT) passages. We will site two here:

Now all who believed were together, and had all things common, and sold their possessions and goods, and divided them among all, as anyone had need. So, continuing daily with one accord in the temple, and breaking bread from house to house, they ate their food with gladness and [singleness] of heart, praising God and having favor with all the people. And the Lord added to the church those who were being saved" (Acts 2:44-47 NKJV).

Now the multitude of those who believed were of one heart and one soul; neither did anyone say that any of the things he possessed was his own, but they had all things in common. And with great power the apostles gave witness to the resurrection of Jesus... (4:32-33 NKJV).

Emerging Themes from the Passages

When you analyze the two preceding passages of Scripture, certain critical themes relevant to true biblical unity emerge; they are as follows:

- The believers belong to a local fellowship and they attended regularly (Heb.10:24-25).
- They did not only attend a fellowship; they were in fellowship with one another (1 John 1:6-7).
- Those that came were on speaking terms with each other, no grudges.
- They were compassionate toward each other; they shared temporalities according to need.
- They were of the same heart and mind (singleness of heart).
- They joyously worshipped together.
- They were loyal to each other and the fellowship.
- The church grew spiritually and numerically (Acts 2:47; 4:33).

The Unique Mission and Structure of the Church

The unique mission and structure of the Church calls for unity. Her mission is global (Matt.28:19-20). Her structure is largely that of a voluntary organization with Jesus as its invisible Spiritual Head, and a local church pastor as the under-shepherd.

All members of the church are called to serve, and without unity the mission cannot be realized; this is where the church is most vulnerable (John 17:20-26). Destructive conflict is a major cause for the exodus of both members and pastors from the church and the ministry. It is also the culprit in most church schisms. Every Christian is called upon to seek peace and pursue it. The challenge is to keep the unity of the Spirit in the bond of peace (Eph.4:1-6).

Discuss five characteristics of the biblical understanding of Christian unity:

1. It is a unity in diversity (1 Cor.3:1-15, 12:13-31).
2. Gifts are recognized and put to work for the common good (1Cor.12:1-12).
3. Unity is impossible without the practice of love (1Cor.13:1-13).
4. Unity requires consistent prayer and the help of the Holy Spirit (Acts1:12-14, 2:1-4).
5. The standard of unity for the church is the quality that binds the Holy Trinity (John 17:20-23).

Discuss the importance of unity to worship and discipleship:

1. Without worship and discipleship, the church has no reason for being.
2. Worship acceptable to God, must be done in the Holy Spirit (John 4:23-24).
3. The Holy Spirit is the true disciple-maker (Acts 2:46-47).

(4) The Holy Spirit does not work well in strife and conflict (Luke 4:14-30; Acts 2:1-2)

Discuss members role in the preservation of unity:

1. Train all members to be gatekeepers of the peace.
2. Train children to be peacekeepers.
3. Inclu91de the peace ministry in the church budget
4. Have your peace ministry build relationships with consultants.
5. Conduct all church peacemakers training regularly.

The Resident Counsel and pastoral relations

The peace ministry of the church is represented by the *Resident Counsel* (RC), or whatever name you give to this team. The RC maintains not only the peace between members but between leadership and members because conflict can develop from both directions.

The *Resident Counsel* has pastoral supervision but is not pastor-led in its day-to-day work. Council members are mature and objective; they understand the pastoral role and know how to maintain the delicate balance. The counsel protects the entire church from destructive conflict; that includes the leadership. When leadership becomes its worst enemy, the RC should objectively step in to bring back balance without usurping the role of the governing boards. When the congregation or certain elements thereof becomes unfair and unreasonable against leadership, the RC stands in the gap to brings back balance.

Lesson Application

The flagship of the peace ministry is unity and knowledge of the word. But unity does not mean there is no disagreement or conflict. We have learned that a healthy, growing congregation will have disagreements and vigorous debate; that's normal conflict.

When the debate is over by reaching a compromise or by majority vote, the fight is also over and in good Christlike spirit. None take up their marbles and go home or take off to cross-town church. It is time for the body to work together in the spirit and bond of unity.

Loyalty to Christ does not trash His church; that is the work of another spirit. Once the matter is decided by the majority or by arbitration, the fight is over. No one or two members and their supporters should hold out and begin a guerrilla warfare against the church of Jesus Christ. The duty of each member is to be a peacemaker and a peacekeeper.

A local church must be at peace with itself to make any impact on the local community. The members must work hard to preserve the reputation of the church to the community.

LESSON 17

CHURCH CONFLICT AND SOCIAL MEDIA

Reading Assignment: (Read textbook Chap.12)

A Word to the Instructor

Corporate unity is critical to the mission of church. In the digital age social media could be the new enemy on the block to preservation of corporate unity. Several pastors and churches have been defamed and their influence and ministry destroyed by reason of social media. Individual members have been shamed and by mean spirited people and the inappropriate use of social media. This lesson is not about how to use social media to extend the ministry reach of the church, but how to safeguard the church and its leaders from social media defamation. It is the duty of all members.

The church must have a written policy with regard to social media; it is not the place for church folks to settle their differences or church business to be posted without authorization. The instructor will lead the class to understand that it is the duty of every member of the church to protect the body of Christ from this new enemy, and it is the responsibility of leadership to ensure that a social media policy is in place in a timely manner.

Lesson Purpose

Social media is a powerful tool for the ministry of the local church in the digital age, but the textbook and this lesson are not dealing with it as a tool of ministry, but as an adversary to guard against as you would fire or conflict. Fire is a useful tool for the comfort of human life, but it is also destructive if it is not properly used, it will get out of our control. In our textbook we say, conflict is like fire, it is useful to any organization, but it can become destructive and become a church's worst nightmare.

Whether your church officially use social media to promote and extend its ministry reach or not, you should not ignore social media, because the people who sit in the pews are using social media platforms and are bringing social media devices to church. Social media can fracture the unity of the local church, defame its leaders, and destroy its ministry influence on the immediate community and the wider world.

Lesson Contents:

As peacemaking is the Christian duty of every member of the church, so is protecting the church from social media defamation. But that will not happen with any measure of seriousness unless the pastor and the governing board lead the way by enacting formal policy measures on the organization's behalf.

Discuss the following headings in light of chapter 12 of the textbook:

- How social media is a double-edged sword
- How church member can wittingly or unwittingly become the cause defamation to their church and the cause of Christ by reason of their social media conduct.
- Simple measures the church can implement now to protect itself from defamation
- How social media becomes a stewardship responsibility for the church.

- Church by-laws and social media influence.

Lesson Application:

Each member of a local church has a covenant relationship with that church and with the Lord of the church to protect His body. It is our Christian duty therefore to conduct ourselves in cyber world and the real world in a Christlike manner.

We should be careful of the content we post on any social media platform, that we are not offensive in language or images posted or what we embrace by clicking like or share or associate our names with. Social media is not the place to take or settle church fights.

People who are not members of the church have no right to the business of the church beyond its redemptive message and work of charity.

LESSON 18

PRETRAINING PHASE

A Word to the Instructor

The five lessons in this section talk directly to students who may one day become instructors themselves. They don't know it yet, but once they have taken this *Basic Training* course, chances are, they will want to teach this course in the future to other church groups and, perhaps, charge a fee for doing so. The time given to the course is a worthy investment.

Since the possibility of students becoming instructors exist, approach training with a broad vision, that students may afterword want to do the *Intermediate* and *Advanced Trainings* that will qualify them to teach the course. For that and other reasons, it makes sense for all students to learn the structure of the course, so they can come up with creative ways to improve its contents and structure. Also, ensure that you the present planners and instructors preserve accurate records of this *Basic Training* for future reference; this includes students' attendance records, scores of quizzes and final exam score as well.

The last three lessons in this section, may appear easy, but bear in mind that planning a training course has many moving parts that the planners have to think through months before the actual training commences. So, encourage students to give attention and creativity to the process; they may come up with new ideas that may serve them well.

Reading Assignment: (Read Textbook – Appendix A)

Lesson Purpose

This lesson discusses some important steps leading up to the *Basic Training* events. Successful training outcomes are not accidental; they are always the result of proper planning. Poor planning is the mother of mediocrity. Training that is properly executed will pay its weight in gold, in terms of rewarding outcomes.

Therefore, allowing enough time to plan and prepare well, is the smartest pretraining investment one can ever make. It has been said, "Perspiration in preparation brings inspiration in presentation." Give yourself enough time to plan well. Ideally, planners should have been thinking about training a year in advance, though this lesson addresses only six months.

Lesson Contents (Basic Training Planning)

A. Six Months Before Basic Training (Vision Implemented).

Discuss five elements to consider in the six-month timeframe before *Basic Training* commences. This discussion assumes the planner (s) have already selected a projected, tentative date for the *Basic Training* to start. If you have not, now is the time to do so. The date chosen can be adjusted during the early weeks of this six-month period. We begin with certain assumptions:

(1) That you are determined to establish a peace ministry at your local church, and you have done some basic research on the subject. The reading of the textbook that leads you to this curriculum is part of that basic research.

(2) That you have made preliminary identification of some materials, such as the textbook you would like to use in the training. The reference section of the textbook points to other helpful materials.

(3) That you have determined that you are going to need a support coalition to properly execute this training. In other words, there is no need to be superman, knocking yourself out to do it alone. Talk to your governing board and lay leaders about your vision and get their support. From those talks you will select qualified, dependable people to form a working coalition (a committee of about 5 to 6 persons).

(3) Brainstorm with your support coalition without wasting time trying to reinvent the wheel. We have already done the heavy lifting and give you a framework to use. Tests your ideas with them, hear theirs. Just ask questions, listen, listen, listen. Take notes! Hear why somethings will work and why others won't. Be opened to suggestions.

(4) From this working coalition you will identify two or three of your most capable people that will help you do the actual teaching. You will assign other tasks to the others.

Give thought to how you are going to finance the *Basic Training*. Are you going to charge a fee? Is the church underwriting the entire training cost? Remember this is not a fundraising event; it is a ministry education event. Students should at least pay for their textbook. But have extra books on hand to loan to those who cannot buy their own.

A docile church may have to be convinced as to why this training is necessary. They probably never had a big fight before, and they cannot see one coming. "Where there is no vision, people perish" (Prov.29:18). They may have to be convinced that calm seas are not enough reason to have no life jacket on board, that a fire extinguisher in the kitchen is not a foolish investment, even though they never had a kitchen fire before.

In the initial discussions about training, one aim is to have coalition members share the pastor's vision for establishing a peace ministry. In fact, it has to become their vision; the more excited they are about it, the better working coalition they will become.

A shared vision is important because establishing a peace ministry should not just be the pastor's baby; the team should adopt this vision and make it their baby as well and help bring it to birth. All through the process, they need to share this feeling of ownership. The team needs to come to understanding that we are in this together. If one-member messes up, the whole team shares the mess; when one wins, they all share the glory.

B. Three Months before Basic Training (Promotion Begins):

Three months before *Basic Training* commences (this is the 2nd half of the 6 months), the pastor and his/her team will begin to fine tune the *Basic Training* protocol. Now, we consider more closely the key issues that the training team should consider; some will take more than others to execute. For example, you may already have your own church building, so all you have to do on item: #1 below is to designate the classroom in terms of the number of people to accommodate.

Review Facility, Date and Time

Make sure your training is not conflicting with any other events in terms of space and time. Is this location or classroom is equipped to accommodate the training?

Promotion: Three months away from training, ramp-up promotion of the training. In addition to the pastor, have key lay leader speak of it. Advertise on bulletin board throughout the building, in weekly church bulletin, send out email blast, call up members. Emphasize early registration and textbook acquisition. Emphasize commencing reading of textbook before class begins.

Sermon Series: The pastor prepares the congregation by preaching a series of sermon (5 minimum) on the Christian duties of peacemaking and peacekeeping, resolving conflict, violence, war and peace. The sermon series is not only educating the church of peacemaking, it is preparing members for what is to come. It helps to get across the importance of them participating in the training to launch the peace ministry.

No matter how hard a pastor tries, you will not have 100% of the membership taking the course; that alone shows the importance of these sermons. A creative pastor may take points from the training and use them for sermons on Sundays before, during and after the training.

Ramp-Up Registration

Assign at least three responsible persons to help with the registration; they should be able to explain a little about the training to people. At every function of the church register people, website registration, registration forms available at the office and strategic location over the building. Registration completed on the spot and returned promptly. Let people know by registering they are also agreeing to the textbook. Registrants collect their textbook, student manual and syllabus. Students commence assigned reading no less than two weeks before class begins. Emphasize doing assigned reading, attendance, and class punctuality.

Curriculum review

No less than two weeks before training starts, pastor and his team meet a few times to discuss the lesson and fine tune preparation for class. At these review meetings (2 or3 at most), the pastor will assign which lessons the other instructors will be teaching.

Plan to give a short quiz on the assigned readings each day the course runs (about 5 questions). The quiz is given before the teaching session begins (it should take about five minutes). The score on the short quizzes will be considered in the final grade score, so keep good record of the scores for each student, attendance record and class participation. Instructors should prepare to be present when the other instructors are teaching, as their support.

Section Review:

Good teaching requires periodic review of the instructors among themselves. Because of time constraint, you may not be able to do this after each lesson, but it can be done after each section. The instructors get together and provide feedback on each lesson presentation. It is critique and praise.

It is a time to be honest with each other in providing feedback to improve performance. If the instructors eye contact was disproportionately to one side of the room, he or she should know that. If the instructor allows one student to monopolize the class, the instructor should be given that information that it does not happen again (the review is a type of teachers meeting. It is for instructors only.

In order for instructors to provide this kind of feedback to each other, when an instructor is teaching, another instructor should be observing and taking notes that will be useful for the instructor's review meeting.

Lesson Summary

Serious work in planning and preparing for the training to come is done during this second three-month period. The team ensures that all the areas of the training to come are covered during this three-month time frame. Registrations are confirmed, materials ordered, including extra textbooks and student manual for the late commers, review the training to come with your group and assign the lessons each instructor will be responsible for.

LESSON 19
THE TRAINING PHASE

Reading Assignment: (Review textbook Chapter 13)

Lesson Purpose

This lesson is not so much for the students as the planners and instructors. But the students need to pay close attention, because some of them are likely to become planners and instructors as well. This lesson looks at the bare bones of the training architecture. It is actually walking through the theory of the training; it is like a musician picking up a music sheet and knows exactly what key to play on the instrument.

First Day of Class

The instructors arrive early, using this precession period to tie up any loose ends, ensure the classroom is comfortable and ready to receive the students, setup any electronic device that will be used during the instruction time. Ensure the temperature of the room is comfortable; ensure there are extra textbooks and student manuals, adequate seating, and so on.

The first day of class is critically important because it sets the stage for the classes to follow. It provides orientation to the course. Students hear what is expected of them, what it takes to complete the course successfully. When students arrive, the instructor covers the following items:

(1) Welcome and Introduction

(2) A short devotion period (prayer)

(3) Review Syllabus (emphasize course expectation)

(4) Students sign attendant sheet

(5) Give short quiz (5 questions on the readings assigned for today[1]

(6) Commence teaching session

If classes are spread out over several days, give a short quiz each day at the beginning of class. If this is just a one-day training, the short quiz might not be necessary. Instruction style varies with lecture, discussion, small groups, audio-visuals, storytelling, question and answer and roleplay.

Review and Evaluation

As you wind down toward the end of the training phase, review some of the critical highlights of the training. For example, the general and biblical tools. Conduct three types of evaluation:

(1) *Instructor's Evaluation of Students:* This evaluation is completed by the instructor on each student to determine if the student meets the requirements of the course as set out in the syllabus. This evaluation includes final exam scores, scores from the short quizzes, attendance, class participation, reading assignments, and other assignments completed. The instructor uses his or her record on each student to make this evaluation. If the instructor did not keep attendant record, quiz record, class participation record, and final exam record, the instructor will have a serious problem honestly

---

[1] During the promotional phase, have registrants commence reading the textbook at least two-weeks before class begins.

evaluating the student. This alone could bring an instructor's integrity into question. So, instructor beware; have a book for this record.

Student that were severely absent from class and did not do the course work will not receive a certificate. To get a certificate without doing the work is not fair to the those that did the work; such certificate would trivialize the entire training. These students may repeat the course when offered again.

(2) *Student's Evaluation of Instructors*: Each student completes an anonymous evaluation of the instructor. The instructor uses this feedback to improve his/her teaching style.

(3) *Student Curriculum evaluation*: Each student completes an evaluation of the entire course, all four sections. This feedback will help to improve the curriculum; the instructor will send it to the author at the email provided.

Class Closing and Graduation

Class closing simple means, the training course has come to an end. The planners thank the students for their participation and congratulate them for completing the course of study.

Those to whom books were loaned will return them, those who purchased books should keep them or give them to the church library. Instructors will secure and file away student records as a school would. This record will be useful to know who to invite to the *Intermediate* and *Advanced* training when it is offered and those who will need to repeat *Basic Training* when it is offered again.

Graduation is the time when those who successfully completed the course are recognized publicly and are awarded their certificate. For some churches, the certificate is awarded at the class closing event, others use the first Sunday morning service after class closing. Other churches set a special ceremony day with food and fellowship to celebrate the occasion. Whatever form you choose, use it as an opportunity to upstage the *peace ministry* of your church. Members that did not take the course of study seriously, need to know that you intend to make your church a peace-loving church and each member a peacemaker.

Members that did not take the course, for whatever reason, may have gotten the message through the sermon series. But those that did not get the sermon series and the course of study, remain a weak link in a peacemaking chain. It takes only one war-loving member to breach the peace.

So, at graduation make a big statement that reinforces the peace ministry of your church, such as: *we are a peace-loving, peacemaking and peacekeeping church; it is our Christian duty. A few of our brothers and sisters have done what they were asked to do and are receiving their certificates today; we congratulate them.* From their number, a few will be appointed to serve on our peace ministry team (*Resident Counsel*). The others will form a pool from which we will draw people to serve on the counsel. These same people that have received their certificate today will now be able to go on to the *Intermediate* and *Advanced* training when it is offered.

Those of you that were not able to take the course this time around, I hope you will take it the next time around; and those of you that started but were not able to complete the course are welcome to repeat it.

LESSON 20

POST-TRAINING & WORK PHASE

Reading Assignment: (Review textbook Chapter 13)

Lesson Purpose

This lesson asks the question, now that I have gone through *Basic Training,* what next? There are few answers to this question. *First,* all persons taking the course will be better able to be a peacemaker and a peacekeeper as their Christian duties as we have already pointed out. Be a person of peace at home, at work, at church and in the marketplaces of this world; it is one of the best ways to represent Jesus Christ.

Second, some of you that receive your certificate will be asked to serve on our peace ministry *Resident Counsel* as *Agent of Peace-Manage of Conflict.* Be the best peacemaker for *the church as you can.* Every member of the church is an agent of peace but council members for a rapid response to deal with the fire of conflict, preventing it from becoming destructive.

Third, successful basic training certificate holders will be able to go on to *Intermediate* and *Advance Training*. Serve Christ will all your mind; be the best scholar you can be.

Fourth, those that started *Basic Training* and were not able to complete it, will be given another chance to repeat the course. This lesson explores these issues.

Remember, *Basic Training* is conducted for the purpose of establishing a peace ministry at the church, your local church, to deal with situations of conflict. We will now consider five essentials for establishing the peace ministry: selection of *Resident Counsel* members, their public charge and consecration, explanation of their ministry function, the work of the counsel, and the next level of training.

Selection of Resident Counsel Members

Depending on size of the church, the authorized leadership selects five to seven (5-7) lay members, who have successfully completed the *Basic Training* and received a certificate. These have also met other qualifications set by the church to serve on the *Resident Counsel*.

A council (*counsel*) member has to be a peace-loving individual, emotionally and spiritually mature, one who understands the mission and purpose of the church. They are appointed as *Agents of Peace-Managers of Conflict* for a three-year term.

Public Charge and Consecration

On the day that the peace ministry is officially launched, the members that were selected to serve on the counsel are set before the congregation and officially charged with the peace ministry of the church. In like manner, the congregation is also charged to respect and honor their ministry to the Body. They are then consecrated to the Lord Jesus Christ for the work.

Since the peace ministry involves the whole church, this event is better done in the Sunday Morning service or at special service called for this purpose. It should be witnessed by a sizable portion of the congregation; it is a teaching moment. The pastor may wrap his/her message around becoming a peace-loving church; use the event to reinforce the peacemaking, peacekeeping Christian duties of each member (Matt.5:9). They must represent Christ everywhere, not as troublemakers but as peacemakers. Every member must know that trashing their church is a work of Satan.

Explanation of the Ministry Function

There are a few members that always miss everything; they were not at church through the weeks of promotion and training. Someone, instructor or person that went through the training will have to explain the ministry function of the *Resident Counsel* to them. It takes only one uninformed member to compromise the peace and fracture unity of a church. This is one chance to get the stragglers on board.

First, let them know counsel is not here to take over the counseling ministry of the church. It is not here to provide marriage counseling to Jack Sprat and his wife on their fight at the Golden Corral over chicken wings. However, if brother Sprat is a deacon of our church, that may be a compromising scandal of interest to the counsel. Officer holders and members that do not represent Christ and His church honorably to the community and the world are of concern to us. Any public behavior by a member that compromises the witness of our church will be is a matter of concern to the Counsel.

Second, following functions fall under the purview of the *Resident Counsel*:

(1) The counsel educates the church on their Christian duties as peacemakers and peacekeepers.

(2) The counsel helps to settle church conflicts in a peaceable and biblical way.

(3) The counsel seeks to preserve the unity of the church from destructive conflict.

(4) The counsel manages destructive conflicts and bring them to resolution, thus preventing conflict from derail the church from its assigned mission.

The counsel seeks to safeguard the integrity of worship and the integrity of its message.

The work of the Resident Counsel (RC)

First, RC must have a space, an office to operate from, a space where it meets regularly. It must be clearly marked as the Office of Peace Ministry. The members have access and confidentiality as deem necessary by the counsel. Busybody people cannot create mischief and use nonsense to clog up RC schedule and expect to hide behind confidentiality.

The work of the counsel is how it carries out its stated function. Throughout the year, the RC conducts trainings, workshop, seminar, sponsor events on peacemaking, peacekeeping, conflict resolution, bullying, workplace violence, domestic violence, and the like.

The RC holds conflict management and resolution sessions (negotiation, mediation, arbitration, prevent expensive litigation); it helps to manage media messaging, referrals for discipline and referral of destructive and unrepentant members for removal (disfellowship, excommunication), it investigates stories in circulation about the church and its leader to protect the integrity of both and clear the record.

Continuing Education Training (CET)

The counsel works closely with the pastoral office in planning the *Intermediate* and *Advanced* levels of training as well as the appropriate time to repeat the *Basic Training*. A small to medium size church may prefer to offer the *Intermediate* level training the year after the *Basic Training, and the Advance Training* a year after the *Intermediate.*

Continuing education training is critical to the peace ministry for three fundamental reasons. *First*, the people who have gone through Basic Training must continue to improve their skills by moving to the higher level of learning. *Second*, a growing church brings in new members and they must be initiated into the peace ministry of the church otherwise they will form a new war zone to undo previous peace effort.

Third, new members must be taught concerning their Christian duties of peacemaking and peacekeeping. They need to be invited to participate in *Basic Training.* By so doing the church continue the add newly trained members to the pool from which to draw members to serve on the *Resident Counsel*. These newly trained members will eventually move to the Intermediate and Advance levels of training. This is how a church maintains a vibrant peace ministry.

Conclusion

As we conclude this *Basic Training* course of study let's emphasize why we should not delay implementing this strategy plan for a peacemaking church:

1. Preserving the unity of the church demands it.

2. Defending the integrity of its message compels it.

3. Not losing the urgency of its mission warrants it.

_____

If you have purchased the textbook or this curriculum, please send the author an email, so we can notify you of upgrades to this curriculum. May the blessings of God be upon you!

Author: MICHAEL W. DEWAR SR., M.Div., LMSW, D.MIN
michaeldewar.com
Send feedback to: Revdewar@gmail.com

APPENDIX A

SYLLABUS AND SCHEDULE

RESOLVING CHURCH AND FAMILY CONFLICT BIBLICALLY

Course Description

This is a six-week intensive course of study, meeting one day each week for four or five hours. Students will be given reading assignments throughout each week. The main curriculum is *Agents of Peace-Managers of Conflicts;* it covers twenty (20) lessons in four sections.

      The course is designed to study the resolution of conflict or peacemaking from a biblical perspective but draws some knowledge base information from nonbiblical sources as well.

      This basic course equips all believers to live out their Christian duties of peace making and peacekeeping. Just as it takes only one careless or malicious person to burn down a million-dollar mansion, so one member can start the fire of conflict that consumes an entire congregation. The ideal thing, therefore, if for every member of the congregation to become an agent of peace by taking this course of study at some point. It is required!

      From among those taking the course, five to seven (5-7) will be chosen to serve as managers of conflict in the peace ministry of the church on a *Resident Council* (RC). The course is also beneficial for anyone wanting to sharpen or acquire skills in personal, family, and workplace conflict management.

This course explores the dynamics of conflict from different practical scenarios. It illustratively defines conflict, helps you understand its causes and patterns, and distinguishes how conflicts are settled in a church organization as opposed to a mere secular organization. The course provides lay leaders and aspiring leaders with the basic practice skills and strategies for resolving conflict biblically.

To complete the course successfully, regular attendance is required, class participation, completing reading assignments, doing the class quizzes, and completing the final exam. The student who satisfactorily completes the course will receive a certificate. Students receiving a certificate may later enroll in the intermediate and advanced levels of training. Student that are not successful may repeat the course the next time it is offered.

The Goals of the Course

1. Discover your preferred conflict management style and learn about other available approaches. Learn how to harness the power of conflict for growth and constructive outcomes. Understand the levels of conflict and learn to identify when a situation is becoming destructive.

2. Understand the dynamics of conflicts, causes and types, and how to resolve them.

3. Learn the five common approaches to dispute resolution and differentiate between biblical and the secular approaches.

4. Learn the fundamental principles of biblical peacemaking.

5. Understand the importance of an intentional, dedicated conflict resolution system in your church and how to go about starting such a ministry.

6. Develop competence in both the social science and biblical approaches to conflict settlement (ten themes on each type will be covered).

Instruction Method

1. Lecture
2. Open class discussion
3. Role Play
4. Case study
5. Group discussion
6. Perhaps a video

Course Competence and Learning Objectives

1. Know the basic categories of conflict resolution
2. Be able to identify the levels of conflict.
3. Know how to resolve conflict biblical.
4. Be better able to analyze, assess, and understand your own response to crisis and conflict, and channel them into meaningful or productive outcomes.
5. Be able to spot conflict being formed and prevent, control, and resolve it.
6. Learn about the role and use of the consultants.
7. Learn about the proper use of arbitration and the court.

Method of Evaluation

1. Class attendance: 20 points per class day (total possible points: 120).

2. Short quiz: (2 points for each correct answer). Possible points per quiz, 10 points.

3. Class participation: 20 Points. Profile exercise 40 points. Luther movie 40 points. Total possible points 100.

4. Assigned reading (10 points per assignment). Total possible 100 points.

5. Final exam, two points for each correct answer (total possible points 160). Final exam passing score is 80 points. A student that receives high scores in all the above areas but falls five points short of passing the final exam shall be given a discretionary pass.

Basic Training Required Texts

Church and Family Conflict by Michael W. Dewar (Available on Amazon.com).
Agents of Peace-Managers of Conflict Student Manual. Agent of Peace-Managers of Conflict curriculum (for instructors only).

Other Helpful Books

Ken Sande, *The Peace Maker: A Biblical Guide to Resolving Personal Conflict,* Third Edition (Grand Rapids, MI: Baker Books, 2004).

Speed B. Leas, *Discovering Your Conflict Management Style* (Bethesda, MD: Alban Institute, 1997).

Alfred Poirier, *The Peacemaking Pastor* (Grand Rapids, MI: Baker Books, 2006).

Desmond Tutu and Mpho Tutu, *The Book of Forgiveness* (New York: Harper Collins, 2014).

COURSE SCHEDULE (SAMPLE)

Planners may use this six-week schedule or make their own. Class meets once each week for four or five hours. Students must start doing the reading assignments two weeks before the first-class session. The exercise is also done at home. Students will get a short quiz at the start of each class.

WEEKS	Curriculum Lessons	Reading Assignments
1	**Introduction to the course** Lesson 1: The Need for a Peace Plan Lesson 2: Discovering your Conflict Style Lesson 3: Your theology of Conflict	1. Read introduction & chapter 1 2. Review chapter 1; Do Exercise in Appendix B of Student Manual. 3. Review theology of conflict in Ch.1; Read chapter 2
2	Lesson 4: Peace as A Christian Duty Lesson 5: Why Churches need to Manage Conflict Effectively Lesson 6: Strategic Peacemaking Plan	4. Read chapter 3 5. Read chapter 4 6. Read chapter 5
3	Lesson 7: Biblical Precedence (OT) Lesson 8: Biblical Precedence (NT) Lesson 9: Historical Precedence (Patristic/Reform.)	7. Read chapter 6 8. Review chapter 7 9. Read chapter 8
4	Lesson 10: Understanding the Nature of Conflict. Lesson 11: Causes and Sources of Conflict. Lesson 12: General Peacemaking Tools (Part 1)	10. Read chapter 9 11: Read chapter 10 12. Read chapter 11
5	Lesson 13: General Peacemaking Tools (Part 2). Lesson 14: Biblical Peacemaking Tools (Part 1). Lesson 15: Biblical Peacemaking Tools (Part 2).	13. Read chapter 11 14. Read chapter 11 (Biblical tools) 15. Read chapter 11 (Biblical tools)
6	Lesson 16: Preserving Corporate Unity Lesson 17: Conflict and Social Media Lesson 18: The Pretraining Phase Lesson 19: The Training Phase Lesson 20: The Post-Training Phase	16. Read assigned Scriptures. 17. Read chapter 12 (Textbook) 18. Read chapter 13 19. Review chapter 13 20. Review chapter 13

APPENDIX B

Your Preferred Conflict Style

Introduction

From the dinner table to the marketplace, people bargain, negotiate and use many approaches to get what they want. The methods that work well for them they tend to use again and again; they are our preferred conflict styles. Most of us don't even know that we have preferred style(s), so we never had the opportunity to analyze it or them. You may be surprised to learn that your style(s) may be the reason or reasons you did or didn't get what you wanted in a conflict or disagreement.

The fact is, there are several approaches that can be consciously used to secure satisfactory outcomes for you and the person(s) you are in conflict with. In this exercise we will help you to uncover your preferred conflict style. It is adopted from, Speed B. Leas' little booklet, *Discovering Your Conflict Management Style (1997). The exercise is best done from the booklet because it has so much more. The naked exercise is placed here in case the booklet is out of print.* The exercise covers six styles but reference is made to more than six.

1. **Persuade**

I try to change my opponent's position, point of view or thinking through persuasive reasoning or argument.

2. Compel

I try to change your opponent's position by using authority, physical force, intimidation or pressure. For example, threat of firing, demotion, suspension of privileges or benefits, lawsuit, police action, subpoena, order of protection and the like.

3. Avoid/Accommodate
I do my best to get away from the situation, even if I have to deny that a problem, disagreement or conflict exist. Or, I accommodate by going along with my opponent, perhaps to preserve the relationship or some other benefits.

4. Collaborate

I invite or agree to sit down with my opponent and work through the problem together.

5. Negotiate

I bargain with my opponent to get a better deal. I will give a little, but I must get something out of this. It is either a win/lose or a win/win outcome.

6. Support

The problem is in the opponent's camp and the opponent needs to take responsibility to fix it, but I will provide some help to fix the problem. For example, your neighbor's dog comes through the fence to do his business on your font lawn. You have a brother-in-law that can fix the fence for your neighbor.

Instructions

The exercise carries 45 questions. Each question has two choices (A and B). Circle the choice that you more closely identify with (A or B, circle only one for each question). There are no right or wrong answers. After you finish answering all 45 questions. Circle your choices exactly on the code sheet. In other words, look at your choices and circle the exact letters (A or B) on the code sheet.

The Exercise Questions

=================

Remember, circle only one choice for each question, the A or the B, not both.

1. A. Using logic, I try to convince the other of my position.
   B. I use whatever authority I have to convince the other of my position.

2. **A.** I let others take responsibility for solving the problem.
   B. I seek the other's help in working out a solution.

3. **A.** I try to find a compromise solution.
   B. I actively listen to the other.

4. **A**. I make an effort to win the other over.
   B. I will make an effort to go along with what the other wants.

5. **A.** I remind the other of the justice of my position.
   B. I show empathy about the other's plight.

6. **A.** I try to surface all of the other person's concerns.
   B. If I give up something, I expect the other to give up something.

7. A. I press my argument to get points made.
   B. I attempt to work on all concerns and issues in the open.
8. **A.** I assert my rights.
   B. I will give up some points in exchange for other.

9. **A.** I try soothe the other's feelings to preserve our relationship.
   B. I encourage the other to act for himself/herself.

10. **A.** I tell the other person my idea.
    B. I propose a middle ground.
11. **A.** I remind the other I am an authority on the subject we are dealing with.
    B. To keep peace, I might sacrifice my own wishes for those of the other.

12. **A.** I invite the other to join me to deal the differences between us.
    B. I assume giving advice creates dependency on me.

13. **A.** I try t show the other the soundness of my position.
    B. I usually repeat back or paraphrase what the other has said.

14. **A.** I use the constitution or policy manual as a backup for my position.
    B. I encourage the other to stay in the conflict with me until we agree.

15. **A.** I try to do what is necessary to avoid tension.
    B. If it makes the other happy, I might let him or her retain some of his or her views.

16. **A.** I point to the consequences if the other doesn't listen.
    B. I am firm in pursuing my argument.

17. **A.** I am concerned with satisfying everybody's wishes.
    B. I try to find a fair way for the other to get what he or she wants.

18. **A.** I don't try to persuade another about what should be done. I help the other find his or her own way.
    B. I try to find a combination of gains and losses for both of us.

19. **A.** I try to postpone the issue until a later time.
    B. I try to show the rationality and benefits of my position.

20. **A.** I am nonjudgmental about what the other says or does.
    B. I call on expert authority to support my case.

21. **A.** I try to find an intermediate position.
    B. I usually seek the other's help in working out a solution.

22. **A.** I tell the other about the problem so we can work it out.
    B. I propose solution to our problem.

23. **A.** I usually as more than I expect to get.
    B. I offer rewards so the others will go along with my point of view.

24. **A.** I try not to give advice, only to help the other make up his or her own mind.
    B. Differences are not always worth worrying about.

25. **A**. I calculate how much I can get, knowing I won't get everything.
    B. I try to gain the other's trust, to get him or her on my side.

26. **A**. I sometimes avoid taking positions that would create unpleasantness.
    B. I withdraw when I don't get my way.

27. **A**. I help the others take care of his or her own problems.
    B. When someone avoids conflict with me, I invite that person to work it out with me.

28. **A**. I try to put a little of myself forward as possible, attempting to make use of the strengths the other.
    B. I point out the faults in the other's arguments.

29. **A**. When someone threatens me, I assume we have a problem and invite that person to work it out with me.
    B. When I am right, I don't argue much, I just state my position and stand firm.

30. **A**. I will give in a little, so everybody gets something he or she wants.
    B. I try not to hurt the other's feelings.

31. **A**. I prepare mu case before joining the argument.
    B. I admonish the other to do as I say.

32. **A**. I am considerate of the other's wishes.
    B. If we are at a loss as to how to work an issue through, we ask for a third party.

33. **A**. To succeed one needs to be flexible.
    B. In a conflict one should focus on fact finding.

34. **A**. I evaluate the positives and negatives of the other's argument.
    B. If the other's position is important to him or her, I would try to meet those wishes.

35. A. It is more important to be right than to be friendly.
   B. I try to help the other feel courage and power to manage his or her own problem.

36. A. I assume we all will be able to come out winners.
   B. I assume conflict management is the art of attaining the possible.

37. A. When opposed, I can usually come up with a counter argument.
   B. I assume we can work a conflict through.

38. A. I emphasize the gravity of the situation,
   B. In a conflict, everybody should come out with something, though not everything that was expected.

39. A. I prefer to postpone unpleasant situations.
   B. I support the other in trying to find his or he way.

40. A. I defend my ideals.
   B. I share only that which is helpful to my case.

41. A. I let others know whether my requirements are being met.
   B. I want the other to be content.

42. A. I attempt to define our mutual problem.
   B. I sympathize with the other's difficulty, but don't take responsibility for them.

43. A. I usually plan out my argument.
   B. I express caring toward the other.

44. A. If it is important, I will put pressure on the other to get what is needed.
   B. I join with the others to gather data about our problem.

45. A. I assume relations are more important than issues.
   B. I assume that each of us must give up something for the good of the whole.

SCORE FORM

Circle the same letter you circle on each item of the questionnaire.

Persuade	Compel	Avoid/ Accommodate	Collaborate	Negotiate	Support
1. A	B				
2.		A	B		
3.				A	B
4. A		B			
5.	A				B
6.			A	B	
7. A			B		
8.	A			B	
9.		A			B
10. A				B	
11.	A	B			
12.			A		B
13. A					B
14.	A		B		
15.		A		B	
16. B	A				
17.		B	A		
18.				B	A
19. B		A			
20.	B				A
21.			B	A	
22. B			A		
23.	B			A	
24.		B			A
25. B				A	
26.	B	A			
27.			B		A
28. B					A
29.	B		A		
30.		B		A	
31. A	B				

#						
32.			A	B		
33.					A	B
34.	A		B			
35.		A				B
36.				A	B	
37.	A			B		
38		A			B	
39.			A			B
40.	A				B	
41.		A	B			
42.				A		B
43.	A					B
44.		A		B		
45.			A		B	

Total: _____|_____|_____|_____|_____ |_____
Enter total number of items circled in each column (Count down from 1 to 45). Each column has 15.

SCORE INTERPRETATION

There is no right or wrong answer. Let's look on the meaning of your scores. On each column of the score sheet, your score can run from a low of 0 (zero) to a maximum of 15 points. The higher your score in any column, the more likely you are using that style in a conflict. The lower your score the less likely you are to us that style. Note, the following two examples:

Fig.1 Jane's Scores

       Style 1: Persuade = 10

       Style 2: Compel = 4

       Style 3: Avoid/accommodate = 5

       Style 4: Collaborate = 12

       Style 5: Negotiate = 7

       Style 6: Support = 7

Jane's highest score is 12 (Collaborate). This suggests she is most comfortable collaborating in a conflicted situation. But note that she scores high on Persuade as well (10). This suggests that this style is a comfortable backup for her. Her low scores are 4 and 5. This suggests that these two styles are more uncomfortable for her in a conflict; she is not likely to use them. She scores 7 on negotiate and 7 on support. This suggest she will have problem choosing one over the other.

If the difference between scores is three points or more, you are likely to hold on longer to the style with the high score, even when it is not getting the job done for you, because you are more comfortable with that approach.

Fig. 2: Henry's scores:

Style 1: Persuade = 3

Style 2: Compel = 2

Style 3: Avoid/accommodate = 2

Style 4: Collaborate = 10

Style 5: Negotiate = 14

Style 6: Support = 14

Henry has two highest score of 14 on negotiate and support. He is most comfortable with these two styles but will have difficulty choosing one over the other. Henry also score 10 on collaborate but may have difficult choosing that style over negotiate and support for which he is more comfortable. Henry is unlikely to choose the three styles for which he has a low score.

Now, tell the class what your scores are. Are you a persuader, collaborator, negotiator or what? This course will help you to become more competent using as many as possible. It you have in your toolkit a wrench for every nut, no job will be too hard for you. Knowledge is power but wisdom is the ability to use knowledge correctly.

APPENDIX C

SHOT QUIZ

Short quiz is given at the very beginning of class for no more than five minutes. They are on the reading assignment. Each right answer values 2 points. Maximum value per test 10 points. Instructors may combine 3 or 4 short quizzes depending on the reading assignment for the class. Circle the correct answer for each question.

****

QUIZ 1: From Textbook Chapter 1

Question 1: My peace theology (or theology of peace) is my personal guiding principle, anchored in Scripture, that governs my attitude toward human conflict, war and violence.

    A. True

    B. False

Question 2: According to chapter 1 of the textbook, which set of three would **NOT** be among the seven ways of settling conflict?

    A. Confronting, avoiding, persuading

    B. Ultimatum, threatening, swearing

    C. Accommodating, collaborating, negotiating

Question 3: The Peace theology of Jesus is best seen:

    A. In the Sermon on the Mount

    B. In His turning water into win.

    C. In the feeding of the five thousand.

Question 4: The peace theology of Jesus is based upon His new commandment to love one another as He loves us:

A. True

B. False

Question 5: The Law of Moses teach that if I knock your eye or tooth out, it is okay for you to demand my eye or tooth to be knocked out in return:

A. False

B. True

QUIZ 2: From Textbook Chapter 2

Question 1: The textbook in chapter 2 talks about three big ideas of peace that we should strive for in our peacemaking effort. Circle the correct set of three below (A, B, or C):

A. Forgiveness, Justice and Restitution, Reconciliation

B. Equal justice, social justice, non-compromise

C. Eye for eye, tooth for tooth, blow for blow

Question 2: According to the Bible, how should you respond to a church brother or sister who holds a grudge against you? (circle the correct answer):

A. Don't talk to that person until he or she comes to talk to you.

B. Discuss it with other church member what a hypocrite this person is.

C. Tell it to the world on Facebook

D. All of the of the above

E. None of the above

Question 3: If a church brother or sister holds a grudge against you, the Bible does not tell you how to handle such personal stuff. You have to find a way to deal with it and hope it's the right way:

A. True

B. False

Question 4: If a church brother or sister is in conflict with you, which of the following you should do:

A. Go to him or her privately and settle it.

B. If he/she refuse to settle it, take one or two witnesses and try again.

C. If he or she still refuse to settle, tell it to the church.

D. All the above

Question 5: When a church member is in enmity with another and refuses to settle, and refuses to submit to the discipline and authority of the church, what should the church do with such member?

A. Just ignore the matter, it will go away.

B. Just let him or her continue to serve in whatever office he or she has, time will take care of it.

C. Suspend all offices held by the person and disfellowship him or her.

QUIZ 3: From Textbook Chapter 3

Question 1: According to chapter 3 of the textbook, the local church needs to manage conflict effectively:

A. Because church "folks like to fight, and they often fight dirty."

B. Because churches have really nice people that don't really fight.

C. Because the Bible says, fight the good fight; fight each other is a good spiritual exercise.

Question 2: All secular enterprises of significance like Google, Apple, General Motors have a system to deal with grievances or conflicts. The church by nature is a unique, voluntary organization of divine origin; as such, she demands a system to prevent conflict from defeating its purpose:

    A. True

    B. False

Question 3: The Holy Spirit resides in each local church, so conflict could never hinder the work of the ministry.

    A. True

    B. False

Question 4: The church needs to manage conflict effectively because:

    A. The church has a global mission of evangelizing the world and conflict can derail that mission.

    B. Conflict creates discord and prevent acceptable worship.

    C. Conflict prevents a church from making disciples of Christ

    D. All the above

Question 5: Unless they repent and love each other, the Holy Spirit can do no great work in a church that is conflicted, and the members are at war among themselves and with their leaders.

    A. True

    B. False

QUIZ 4: From Textbook Chapter 4

According to Chapter 4 of the textbook the local church needs a strategic conflict resolution or peacemaking plan with five components. Each of the next five questions deal with one component; try to identify it.

Question 1: The peacemaking plan should be Biblically based

    A. True

    B. False

Question 2: The peacemaking plan should be residentially situated (at the local church)

    A. True

    B. False

Question 3: The peacemaking plan should be educationally intended. It is designed to educate all members of the church, including children.

    A. True

    B. False

Question 4: The local church peacemaking plan should be led by lay-leaders.

    A. False

    B. True

Question 5: The local church peacemaking plan or ministry should have pastoral oversight or supervision.

    A. True

    B. False

QUIZ 5: From Textbook Chapter 5

We all know about legal precedence, where a prosecutor searches the law books to find a case that provides guidance for the case at hand. In like manner, we search the scriptures to see how God dealt with conflicts in the Old New Testaments for guidance on dealing with conflicts today.

Question 1: (Circle the right answer, A or B)
How did God handle His first conflict with the human family? This is His conflict with Adam and Eve.

- A. God gave them what they deserve, punish them without mercy, and drove them from the garden.
- B. He dealt with them in love and mercy, not taking their lives but used an animal to atone for their sins.

Question 2: God turning Adam and Eve out of the garden was:

- A. Unfair, even cruel and unusual punishment because the garden was their home.
- B. An act of love and mercy because had they eaten from the Tree of Life and live forever in their sinful state; that would have been living hell for all humans.

Question 3: The conflict between Cain and his brother ended in murder. This happened over worship and after worship. Cain was unrepentant. God did not take Cain's life for his brother's life. What is God teaching us about conflict management and resolution?

- A. He is teaching us that He is a God of equal Justice.
- B. He is teaching us that He is a God of justice, but justice must be restrained by mercy.

Question 4: The conflict between Abraham and his nephew Lot, teaches what about resolving conflict?

- A. That the ultimate aim of Christian conflict settlement is to please God.
- B. That we should strive to preserve the relationship when settling conflict.

C. That we should not only look to our own interest but to the interest of others also.

D. All the above

Question 5: Throughout this study we will be talking about lay people leading the peace ministry, settling conflicts in the local church, not the pastor assuming all that responsibility. Is there any precedence for this approach in the Old Testament? If so, who introduce it to the people of God.

A. Adam and Eve

B. Abraham and Lot

C. Jethro and Moses

QUIZ 6: From Textbook Chapter 6

Question 1: According to Chapter 6 of the textbook the New Testament teaches that conflict must be settled in the house. The expression "in the house" means that:

A. Church folks must settle their disagreements in a Christlike way among themselves.

B. Church folks must first take their disputes to the secular courthouse.

C. Whatever way you can find people to agree with your side of a story take it.

Question 2: The first major conflict faced by the New Testament Church was over:

A. Which apostle should be the head Bishop

B. Unfairness in the distribution of food to widows

C. Whether Jesus literally mean to put away the sword

Question 3: The first major conflict faced by the early church; the apostles had to:

  A. Take time off from the ministry of the word to resolve it.

  B. Appoint a team of lay leaders to resolve the conflict.

  C. The apostles were so overwhelmed, they were scattered abroad.

Question 4: The Stephen-Phillip Dispute Resolution Counsel best reminds us of:

  A. How Cain and Able dispute was settled

  B. How Abraham and Lot dispute was settled

  C. How Moses settled dispute after his father-law counseled him.

Question 5: This evangelistic team broke up because of a sharp dispute over a family member:

  A. Paul and Silas

  B. Paul and Barnabas

  C. Peter and John Mark

QUIZ 7: From Textbook Chapter 7

Question 1: When we talk about the Patristic Period, we mean the period of the Church Fathers which runs from about the ending of the first century to about 450 AD:

  A. True

  B. False

Question 2: The Patristic Period is also called:

  A. The post-apostolic period

  B. The post-medieval period

  C. The post reformation period

Question 3: Which Roman leader ended persecution and made Christianity the religion of the state?

 A. Emperor Nero

 B. Emperor Constantine

 C. The Caesars

Question 4: When secular Rome fell, what institution took the reins of government?

 A. The Jewish Sanhedrin

 B. The Western Church

 C. The Herodian line of kings

Question 5: The council of Nicaea was convened by Emperor Constantine 325 AD to settle doctrinal disputes in the church.

 A. False

 B. True

QUIZ 8: From Textbook Chapter 8

Question 1: Conflict is like fire:

 A. Because both serve you well when they are under control

 B. because both can be managed

 C. Because both could be destructive when out of control

 D. All the above

 E. None of the above

Question 2: Conflict is like Hurricane:

A. Because they both have five stages

B. Because they are both uncontrollable

Question 3: Conflict is like cancer because they both have progressive levels or stages

    A. True

    B. False.

Question 4: Which statement is right, conflict is:

    A. Destructive conflict is preventable

    B. Conflict is manageable

    C. Conflict is resolvable

    D. All the above

    E. None of the above

Question 5:

Keeping the peace at the local church is the duty of every church member

A. True

B. False

QUIZ 9: From Textbook Chapter 9

Question 1: According to textbook Chapter 9 on *"Causes and Sources"* **which of the following is a cause of church conflict:**

    A. People fight over values and beliefs

    B. People fight because of unclear structures

    C. Pastor's role and responsibilities

    D. All the above

Question 2: Which of the following is **NOT** discussed as a cause of church conflict:

A. Loyalty to church tradition

B. New pastor making sudden sweeping changes

C. Dictatorial leadership

D. The church paying monthly stipend the previous pastor

Question 3: Some pastors behave abusively toward their congregations because of undiagnosed mental health problems, and some members behave abusively toward pastors for the same reason.

A. True

B. False

Question 4: Pastors who are frequently in the hearth of conflict are likely to become unhealthy by burnout and prematurely end their pastoral tenure.

A. True
B. False

Question 5: Though often overlooked, both pastor and congregation need according to Eph. 5:21 need to submit to each under Christ.

A. False

B. True

QUIZ 10: From Textbook Chapter 10

Question 1: According to chapter 10 of the textbook, there are ten general tools or principle used by both secular and Christian disciplines to resolve disputes, but for Christians use the differently from the secular discipline because our values are different.

A. True

B. False

Question 2: Which of the following is **NOT** a tool or principle used to resolve conflict?

    A. Prevention
    B. Avoidance
    C. Negotiation
    D. Sarcasm

Question 3: To negotiate is to bargain
    A. True
    B. False

Question 4: Which of the following is **NOT** a tool or principle used to settle conflict?
    A. Mediation
    B. Accommodation
    C. Collaboration
    D. Transition

Question 5: Which of the following is **NOT** a conflict resolution principle or tool?
    A. Reconciliation
    B. Arbitration
    C. Litigation
    D. Conformation

QUIZ 11: From Textbook Chapter 11

Question 1: There are ten biblical principles given in chapter 11 of the textbook that are used with the ten secular principles of chapter 10 which of the following is not among them?

    A. Repentance

    B. Confession

    C. Forgiveness

    D. Justification

Question 2: Which of the following is not among the biblical principle to resolve conflict?

    A. Sanctification

    B. Reconciliation

    C. Restitution

    D. Christian love

Question 3: Which of the following is not a tool used in settling church conflict

    A. Taking the interest of others into consideration

    B. Using the authority of the Church and scripture to discipline

    C. Disfellowshipping the unrepentant member

    D. Chastise the individual member from the pulpit.

Question 4: According to the Bible, the church has the power to hand over the unrepentant member over to Satan for discipline.

    A. True

    B. False

Question 5: When a member id disciplined or disfellowship from the church, the church's responsibility toward that member has ended.

    A. True

    B. False

QUIZ 12
Base on Textbook Chapters 12 &13

Question 1: To protect the church from defamation in the digital age, the pastor and governing board should take the lead enacting a social media policy to protect the organization.
  A. True
  B. False

Question 2: Since just about all members of the church and visitors to the church possess a social media reporting device and are likely to post content and images, it is the duty of all members to protect the church from social media defamation.
  A. True
  B. False

Question 3: The social media policy of the church should at least be reflected in the church's by-laws.
  A. True
  B. False

Question 4: Just about every business or enterprise of significance has a social media policy as to how leaders, staff and employees should conduct themselves on the use of social media platforms.
  A. True
  B. False

Question 5: The minimum time to train workers and launch a peace ministry at your church is:
  A. Three months
  B. Sixth months
  C. Twelve months

_____

See answer key next page.

SHORT QUIZ ANSWER KEYS (SQAK)

(Two points for each correct answer, 10 per quiz. Total possible points, 120)

QUIZ 1: From chapter 1 of the textbook

- Question 1 answer: (A) True
- Question 2 answer: (B)
- Question 3 answer: (A)
- Question 4 answer: (A) True
- Question 5 answer: (B) True

QUIZ 2: From textbook Chapter 2

- Question 1 answer: (A)
- Question 2 answer: (E) None of the above
- Question 3 answer: (B) False
- Question 4 answer: (D) All of the above
- Question 5 answer: (C)

QUIS 3: From textbook Chapter 3

- Question 1 answer: (A)
- Question 2 answer: (A) True
- Question 3 answer: (B) False
- Question 4 answer: (D) All the above
- Question 5 answer: (A) True

QUIZ 4: From textbook Chapter 4
- Question 1 answer: (A) True
- Question 2: answer: (A) True

- Question 3 answer: **(A) True**

- Question 4 answer: **(B) True**

- Question 5 answer: (A) True

QUIZ 5: From Textbook Chapter 5
- **Question 1 answer: (B)**

- **Question 2 answer:** (B)

- **Question 3 answer: (B)**

- **Question 4 answer: (D) All the above**

- **Question 5 answer: (C)** Jethro and Moses

QUIZ 6: From textbook Chapter 6
- **Question 1 answer: (A)**

- **Question 2 answer: (B)**

- **Question 3 answer: (B)**

- **Question 4 answer: (C)**

- **Question 5 answer: (B)**

QUIZ 7: From Textbook Chapter 7
- **Question 1 answer: (A) True**

- **Question 2 answer: (A)**

- **Question 3 answer: (B)**

- **Question 4 answer: (B)**

- **Question 5 answer: (B) True**

QUIZ 8: From Textbook Chapter 8
- **Question 1 answer: (D) All the above**

- **Question 2 answer: (A)**

- **Question 3 answer: (A) True**

- Question 4 answer: (D) All the above

- Question 5 answer: (A) True

QUIZ 9: From Textbook Chapter 9
- Question 1 answer: (D) All the above
- Question 2 answer: (D)
- Question 3 answer: (A) True
- Question 4 answer: (A) True
- Question 5 answer: (B) True

- **QUIZ 10: From textbook Chapter 10**

- Question 1 answer: (A) True

- Question 2 answer: (D)

- Question 3 answer: (A) True)
- Question 4 answer: (D)
- Question 5 answer: (D)

QUIZ 11: From textbook Chapter 11
- **Question 1 answer: (D)**

- **Question 2 answer: (A)**

- **Question 3 answer: (D)**

- **Question 4 answer: (A) True**

- **Question 5 answer: (B) False**

Name of Student: _____ Date: _____

FINAL EXAM

In this exam, read the question carefully then circle the letter that is the right answer. Two points for each correct answer. Total possible points 160.

=================

Question 1: According to the Bible, the church is "the family of God." If that is true, destructive church conflict is a *dirty family fight*:
   A.   False

   B.   True

Question 2: My peace theology or theology of peace is my personal guiding principle, anchored in Scripture, that governs my attitude toward human conflict, war and violence.
   A.   True
   B.   False

Question 3: Which set of three is **NOT** among the seven popular ways of settling conflict?
   A.   Confronting, avoiding, persuading

   B.   Ultimatum, threatening, swearing

   C.   Accommodating, collaborating, negotiating

Question 4: The Peace theology of Jesus is best seen:
   A.   In the Sermon on the Mount.

   B.   In His turning water into win.

   C.   In His feeding of the five thousand.

Question 5: The peace theology of Jesus is based upon:
   A.   His new commandment to love one another as He loves us.

B. Upon the Law of Moses

C. Upon our good human nature.

Question 6: The Law of Moses teach that if I knock your eye or tooth out, it is okay for you to demand my eye or tooth to be knocked out in return:
   A. False

   B. True

Question 7: According to our textbook, there are three big ideas of peace that we should strive for in our peacemaking effort. Circle the correct set of three below (A, B, or C):
   A. Forgiveness, Justice and Restitution, Reconciliation

   B. Equal justice, social justice, non-compromise

   C. Eye for eye, tooth for tooth, blow for blow

Question 8: According to the Bible, how should you respond to a church brother or sister who holds a grudge against you? (circle the correct answer):
   A. Don't talk to that person until he or she comes to talk to you.

   B. Discuss it with other church member what a hypocrite this person is.

   C. Tell it to the world on Facebook.

   D. None of the above

   E. All of the above

Question 9: If a church brother or sister holds a grudge against you, the Bible does not tell you how to handle such personal stuff. You have to find a way to deal with it and hope it's the right way.

   A. True

   B. False

Question 10: If a church brother or sister is in conflict with you, which of the following you should do?

    A. Go to him or her privately and settle it.

    B. If he or she refuse to settle it, take one or two witnesses and try again.

    C. If he or she still refuse to settle, tell it to the church.

    D. All the above

Question 11: When a church member is in enmity or conflict with another and refuses to settle, and also refuses to submit to the discipline and authority of the church, what should the church do?

    A. Just ignore the whole thing, it will go away.

    B. Just let him or her continue to serve in whatever office he or she has, time will take care of it.

    C. Suspend all offices held by the member and disfellowship him or her from the church.

Question 12: There are several important ideas to consider when working for peace; which of the following is **NOT** one of them:

    A. Working for forgiveness

    B. Working for justice and restitution

    C. Working to keep troublemakers away from the pastor

    D. Working for reconciliation

Question 13: According to our textbook, the local church needs to manage conflict effectively

    A. Because church "folks do fight, and they often fight dirty."

    B. Because churches have really nice people that don't really fight.

    C. Because the Bible says, fight the good fight; fight is a good spiritual exercise.

Question 14: All secular enterprises of significance like Google, Apple, General Motors have a system to deal with grievances or conflicts. The church by nature is a unique, voluntary organization of divine origin; as such, it demands a system to prevent conflict from defeating its purpose.

    A. True

    B. False

Question 15: The Holy Spirit resides in each church, so conflict could never hinder the ministry work.

    A. True

    B. False

Question 16: The church needs to manage conflict effectively because:

    A. Conflict will derail it from its global mission of evangelization.

    B. Conflict creates discord and prevents acceptable worship.

    C. Conflict prevents a church from making authentic disciples for Christ.

    D. All the above

Question 17: Unless they repent and love each other, the Holy Spirit can do no great work in a church that is conflicted, and the members are at war among themselves and with their leaders.

    A. True

    B. False

Question 18: Each local church needs a peacemaking plan that is Biblically based

    A. True

    B. False

Question 19: The peacemaking plan of the local church should be residentially situated:

A. **True**

B. **False**

Question 20: The peacemaking plan of the local church should be educationally intended, designed to educate all members of the church, including children.

A. **True**

B. **False**

Question 21: According to our textbook, the peacemaking plan or ministry of the local church should be led by lay-leaders, not the pastor.

A. **False**

B. **True**

Question 22: According to our textbook, the peacemaking plan or ministry of the local church should have pastoral supervision.

A. True

B. False

Question 23: God turning Adam and Eve out of the garden was:
A. Unfair, even cruel and unusual punishment because the garden was their home.
B. An act of love and mercy because had they eaten from the Tree of Life and live forever in their sinful state; that would have been living hell for all humans.

Question 24: The conflict between Cain and his brother ended in murder. This happened over worship and after worship. Cain was unrepentant. God did not take Cain's life for his brother's life. What is God teaching us about conflict management and resolution?
A. He is teaching us that He is the God of equal Justice.

B. He is teaching us that He is the God of justice, but justice must be restrained by mercy.

Question 25: The conflict between Abraham and his nephew Lot, teaches what about resolving conflict?

    A. That the ultimate aim of Christian conflict settlement is to please God.

    B. That we should strive to preserve the relationship when settling conflict.

    C. That we should not only look to our own interest but to the interest of others also.

    D. All the above

Question 26: Which of the following stories about conflict best reflect a lay leadership approach to conflict settlement for the local church?

    A. Adam and Eve conflict with God

    B. Abraham and Lot conflict

    C. The plan Jethro gave to Moses

Question 27: According to the textbook, the New Testament teaches that conflict must be settled in the house. The expression "in the house" means that:

    A. Church folks must settle their disagreements in a Christlike way among themselves.

    B. Church folks must first take their disputes to the secular courthouse.

    C. Whatever way you can find people to agree with your side of a story take it.

Question 28: The first major conflict faced by the New Testament Church was over:

    A. Which apostle should be the head Bishop?

B. Unfairness in the distribution of food to widows.

C. Whether Jesus literally mean for us to put away the sword

Question 29: The first major conflict faced by the early church; the apostles had to:

A. Take time off from the ministry of the word to resolve it.

B. Appoint a team of lay leaders to resolve the conflict.

C. The apostles were so overwhelmed, they were scattered abroad.

Question 30: The Stephen-Phillip Dispute Resolution Counsel best reminds us of:

A. How Cain and Able dispute was settled

B. How Abraham and Lot dispute was settled

C. How Moses settled dispute after his father-law counseled him.

Question 31: Following evangelistic team broke up because of a sharp dispute over a family member:

A. Paul and Silas

B. Paul and Barnabas

C. Peter and John Mark

Question 32: When we talk about the Patristic Period, we mean the period of the Church Fathers which runs from about the ending of the first century to about 450 AD.

A. True

B. False

Question 33: The Patristic Period is also called

A. The post-apostolic period

B. The post-medieval period

C. The post reformation period

Question 35: Which Roman leader made Christianity the religion of the state?

    A. Emperor Nero

    B. Emperor Constantine

    C. The Caesars

Question 36: When secular Rome fell, what institution took the reins of government?

    A. The Jewish Sanhedrin

    B. The Western Church

    C. The Herodian line of kings

Question 37: The council of Nicaea was convened by Emperor Constantine 325 AD to settle doctrinal disputes in the church.

    A. False

    B. True

Question 38: Conflict is like fire:

    A. Because both serve you well when they are under control.

    B. Because both can be managed, if properly planned for.

    C. Because both could be destructive when out of control.

    D. All the above

    E. None of the above

Question 39: Conflict is like Hurricane:

    A. Because they both have five stages

    B. Because they are both uncontrollable

Question 40: Conflict is like cancer because they both have progressive levels or stages

    A. True

    B. False.

Question 41: Which statement is right, conflict is:
    A. Destructive conflict is preventable

    B. Conflict is manageable

    C. Conflict is resolvable

    D. All the above

    E. None of the above

Question 42: Keeping the peace at the local church is the duty of:
    A. The Pastor only

    B. The duty of the deacons only

    C. The duty of all the members

Question 43: According to the textbook which of the following is a cause of church conflict:
    A. People fight over values and beliefs

    B. People fight because of unclear structures

    C. People fight over Pastor's role and responsibilities

    D. All the above

    E. None of the above

Question 44: Which of the following is **NOT** discussed as a cause of church conflict:
    A. Loyalty to church tradition

    B. New pastor making sudden sweeping changes

    C. Dictatorial leadership

D. The church paying monthly stipend the previous pastor

Question 45: Some pastors behave abusively toward their congregations because of undiagnosed mental health problems, and some members behave abusively toward pastors for the same reason.
A. True

B. False

Question 46: Pastors who are frequently in the hearth of conflict are likely to become unhealthy by burnout and prematurely end their pastoral tenure.
A. True
B. False

Question 47: Though often overlooked, both pastor and congregation need to submit to each other under Christ, according to Ephesians 5:21:
A. False

B. True

Question 48: According to the textbook, there are ten general tools or principles used by both secular and Christian practitioners to resolve disputes, but Christians use the differently because the operate on a different set of values:
A. True
B. False

Question 49: Which of the following is **NOT** a tool or principle used to resolve conflicts?
A. Prevention
B. Avoidance
C. Negotiation
D. Sarcasm

Question 50: To negotiate is to bargain
   A. True
   B. False

Question 51: Which of the following is **NOT** a tool or principle used to settle conflict?
   A. Mediation
   B. Accommodation
   C. Collaboration
   D. Transition

Question 52: Which of the following is **NOT** a conflict resolution principle or tool?
   A. Reconciliation
   B. Arbitration
   C. Litigation
   D. Conformation

Question 53: There are ten biblical principles given in the textbook that are used with the ten secular principles. Which of the following is not among them?

   A. Repentance

   B. Confession

   C. Forgiveness

   D. Justification

Question 54: Which of the following is not among the biblical principle to resolve conflict?

   A. Sanctification

   B. Reconciliation

   C. Restitution

   D. Christian love

Question 55: Which of the following is not a tool used in settling church conflicts:

A. Taking the interest of others into consideration

B. Using the authority of the Church and scripture to discipline

C. Disfellowshipping the unrepentant member

D. Chastise the individual member from the pulpit.

Question 56: According to the Bible, the church has the power to hand over the unrepentant member over to Satan for discipline.

A. True

B. False

Question 57: When a member is disciplined by disfellowshipping him or her from the church, the church's responsibility toward that member over:

A. True

B. False

Question 58: The Bible teaches that a member that is overtaken a fault or falls into sin—those that are spiritually strong or mature should seek to restore that member to fellowship. What would be necessary to restore a disfellowship member to fellowship?

A. The member must show evidence that he or she has repented of the situation that caused him or her to be disfellowshipped

B. The member must pay up all back dues or tithes first to be restored to fellowship.

C. Once a troublemaker is dropped from the church he or she should never be reinstated.

59. Which of the following is **not** one of the five most common ways of settling disputes:

A. Mediation

B. Negotiation

C. Council of Baptist Bishops

D. Litigation

E. Arbitration

60. According to the Bible, which of the following is of greater priority in peacemaking?

A. First, go and pay your tithes.

B. First, go and be reconciled to the offender.

C. First, go and take Holy Communion.

D. First, go and restore things taken dishonestly.

61. Negotiation is:
A. A bargaining process used to reach mutual agreement in a dispute.
B. A tool used in conflict to outsmart your opponent.
C. Standing your ground in a conflict to win without giving in.
D. A conflict tactic never to compromise if you want to win.

62. Mediation is best understood as:
A. Taking the middle ground in a dispute.
B. A type of negotiation in which the two sides in a dispute mutually agree to bring in a neutral third party to help them settle the dispute.
C. A facilitator siding with one party to gain the advantage.
D. A type of negotiation in which third parties argue their own interests

63. Arbitration is:
A. A select body of individuals who consider the evidence presented in a dispute and render a binding decision that is almost always upheld legally.
B. Two or more individuals who negotiate with disputing parties.
C. A group that argues for a win-win outcome in a dispute that is nonbinding.
D. A paid group of lawyers arguing for advantage in a dispute.

64. Litigation is:
   A. Settling a dispute in a court of law.
   B. When individuals settle their disputes with a third-party present.
   C. When individuals with the help of their pastor do the right thing.
   D. When the official board of a church gives a ruling in a dispute.

65. Genuine confession includes
   A. Acknowledge the hurt
   B. Accept the consequences
   C. Alter your behavior
   D. All the above
   E. None of the above

66. Which of the following is a key step in confession?
   A. Demand your rights until you get them.
   B. Don't admit to wrong until others admit to theirs.
   C. Ask for forgiveness (and allow time for it).
   D. Confess only to God.

67. Choose the correct answer below:
   A. Forgiveness is the good feeling that signals to let go of my grudges.
   B. Forgiveness is forgetting the hurt inflected on me.
   C. Forgiveness is a decision I make to let go of grudges and the need to retaliate.
   D. Forgiveness is none of the above.

68. Restitution is the biblical concept of giving back material property taken by fraud from its owner. If one has truly repented, restitution has to be considered in the conflict settlement:
   A. True
   B. False

69. In conflict **prevention**, the peacemaker functions as a:
   A. Provider
   B. Teacher
   C. Bridge-builder
   D. Referee

E. A, B and C

70. In **resolving** conflict, the peacemaker plays the role of:
    A. Mediator
    B. Arbiter
    C. Equalizer
    D. Healer
    E. All of the above

71. The textbook preferred name for the local church peace ministry is, *Resident Counsel:*
    A. True
    B. False

72. Launching a *Resident Counsel* at the local church involves three panning phases—pretraining, training, and post-training:
    A. True
    B. False

73. The textbook preferred peace ministry model is:
    A. A pastor-led approach
    B. A lay-leaders' approach

74. When a member is disfellowshipped from a church, the church immediately has no responsibility toward that member.
    A. True
    B. False

75. What is the Christlike response toward any member is excommunicated member:
    A. Continue to isolate and shame him or her as long as possible.
    B. Continue discipleship work leading to restoration.
    C. Publish his or her failings on Facebook so he does do it again.

76. To protect the church from defamation in the digital age, the pastor and governing board should take the lead enacting a social media policy to protect the organization.
    C. True
    D. False

77. Since just about all members of the church and visitors to the church possess a social media reporting device and are likely to post content and images, it is the duty of all members to protect the church from social media defamation.
    C. True
    D. False

78. The social media policy of the church should at least be reflected in the church's by-laws.
    C. True
    D. False

79. Just about every business or enterprise of significance has a social media policy as to how leaders, staff and employees should conduct themselves on the use of social media platforms.
    C. True
    D. False

80. Church members bringing their disputes to social media is not fitting with the biblical way of settling church conflict.
    A. True
    B. False

See answer code in Appendix E next. The answers to the Final Exam are not collected in one place for the Student Manual as they are in the Instructor's Manual.

APPENDIX E

FINAL EXAM ANSWER CODE

The letter in parenthesis is the correct answer. Words to the right help to explain the answer. If explanation is confusing, check the test question. Each right answer values two points, total possible points 160. Passing grade 80 points. 80 Passing. 81 to 95 Good. 96 to 150 Excellent. 151 to 160 Superior

==============

Question 1: (B.) True - According to the Bible, the church is the family of God; therefore, destructive church conflict is a *dirty family fight*.

Question 2: (A.) True – My theology of peace is my personal guiding principle, anchored in scripture that governs my attitude toward conflict, war and violence.

Question 3: (B.) Ultimatum, threatening, swearing are not among the 7 ways of settling conflict.

Question 4: (A.) In the Sermon on the Mount.

Question 5: (A.) His new commandment to love one another as He loves us.

Question 6: (B.) True – The Law of Moses teach an eye for an eye, and a tooth for a tooth.

Question 7: (A.) Forgiveness, Justice and Restitution, Reconciliation are the three big ideas the textbook says we should strive for in our peacemaking effort.

Question 8: (D.) None of the above – these are **Not** the ways to respond to church brother or sister with a grudge against you.

Question 9: (B.) False – The Bible gives clear direction on handling someone with a grudge against you.

Question 10: (D.) All the above (see the question).

Question 11: (C). Suspend all offices held by the member and disfellowship him or her from the church (the member is unrepentant and refuses to submit to the authority of the church).

Question 12: (C.) Working to keep troublemakers away from the pastor.

Question 13: (A.) Because church "folks do fight, and they often fight dirty."

Question 14: (A.) True – The church demands a system to prevent conflict from defeating its purpose.

Question 15: (B.) False – Conflict can prevent the Holy Spirit from effectively working with a church.

Question 16: (D.) All the above (see the question).

Question 17: (A.) True – The Holy Spirit can do no great work in a hateful, conflicted church.

Question 18: (A.) True – Each church needs a biblical peacemaking plan.

Question 19: (A.) True – The peacemaking plan should be residential (based at the local church).

Question 20: (A.) True – The peace plan is to educate the entire church, including children.

Question 21: (B.) True – The peace ministry should be led by lay members.

Question 22: (A.) True – The peace ministry must have pastoral oversight or supervision.

Question 23: (B.) An act of love and mercy God turning Adan and Eve out of the garden.

Question 24: (B.) He is teaching us that He is the God of justice, but justice must be restrained by mercy.

Question 25: (D.) All the above (see the question).

Question 26: (C.) The plan Jethro gave to Moses.

Question 27: (A.) – Church folks must settle their conflict among themselves in a Christlike way.

Question 28: (B.) Unfairness in the distribution of food to widows (Acts 6:1-7).

Question 29:(B.) Appoint a team of lay leaders to resolve the conflict (Acts 6:1-7)

Question 30: (C.) How Moses settled dispute after his father-law counseled him.

Question 31: (B.) Paul and Barnabas (evangelistic team broke up in dispute).

Question 32: (A. True). Patristic Period - ending of the first century to about 450 AD.

Question 33: (A.) The patristic period is also called the post-apostolic period.

Question 35: (B). Emperor Constantine made Christianity the State Religion.

Question 36: (B.) The Western Roman Church

Question 37: (B.) True. (The council of Nicaea was convened by Emperor Constantine 325 AD to settle doctrinal disputes in the church).

Question 38: (D.) All the above (see the question).

Question 39: (A.) Conflict is like hurricane because they both have five stages.

Question 40: (A.) True. Conflict is like cancer because they have progressive levels or stages.

Question 41: (D.) All the above (see the question).

Question 42: (C.) The duty of all the members (to keep the peace at the local church).

Question 43: (D.) All the above (see the question).

Question 44: (D.) Paying monthly stipend to the previous pastor (**NOT** discussed as a cause of conflict).

Question 45: (A.) True. (Some pastoral abusive and some members abuse of pastors stems from undiagnosed mental health problems).

Question 46: (A.) True. (Pastors who are frequently in the hearth of conflict are likely to become unhealthy by burnout and prematurely end their pastoral tenure).

Question 47: (B.) True. Both pastor and congregation are called to submit to each other under Christ, according to Ephesians 5:21)

Question 48: (A.) True (Ten general tools used to settle disputes).

Question 49: (D.) Sarcasm. (**NOT** a tool or principle used to resolve conflicts).

Question 50: (A.) True. (To negotiate is to bargain).

Question 51: (D.) Transition. (**NOT** a tool or principle used to settle conflict).

Question 52: (D.) Conformation. (NOT a conflict resolution principle or tool).

Question 53: (D) Justification. (Not a biblical principle for resolving conflicts).

Question 54: (A) Sanctification. (Not a biblical principle to resolve conflict).

Question 55: (D) Chastising individual member from the pulpit (**Not** a conflict settling tool).

Question 56: (A)True. (The church can hand you over to Satan for discipline).

Question 57: (B) False. (A church's responsibility is **Not** over after it disfellowships a member).

Question 58: (A). (One must show evidence of repentance to be restored to disfellowship).

Question 59: (C) Council of Baptist Bishops. (Not a common way of settling disputes).

Question 60: (B) First, go and be reconciled to the offender. (A greater the priority in peacemaking).

Question 61: (A) (Negotiation is: A bargaining process used to reach mutual agreement in a dispute).

Question 62: (B) Mediation is: (A type of negotiation in which the two sides in a dispute mutually agree to bring in a neutral third party to help them settle the dispute).

Question 63: (A) (Arbitration: An independent body that renders a binding decision in a dispute.

Question 64: (A) (Litigation is: Settling a dispute in a court of law).
Question 65: (D) All the above (see the question).
Question 66: (C) Ask for forgiveness (and allow time for it).
Question 67: (C) Forgiveness is a decision I make to let go of grudges and the need to retaliate.
Question 68: (A) True – Restitution should be considered in conflict settlement.
 Question 69: (E) A, B and C (see the question).
Question 70: (E) All of the above (see the question).
Question 71: (A) True – *Resident Counsel* is the textbook preferred name for the church peace ministry.
Question 72: (A) True – Launching a Resident Counsel...involves three phases....
Question 73: (B) A lay-leaders' approach
Question 74: (B) False –The church has responsibility toward a disfellowshipped member.

Question 75: (B) Continue discipleship work leading to restoration.
Question 76: (A) True

Question 77: (A) True

Question 78: (A) True

Question 79: (A) True

Question 80: (B) Sixth months

APPENDIX F

STUDENT'S EVALUATION OF INSTRUCTOR

Use this form to give your candid and honest evaluation of the instructor.
The evaluation is anonymous, so you are not required to put your name on it.
Complete one for each instructor. Circle your answer and put **X** on the line under your
answer.

1. Concerning the subject, the instructor came across as one who is:

Not informed · Somewhat informed · Informed · Very informed

_____   _____   _____   _____

2. Were the themes discussed made clear to your understanding?

Not clear · Somewhat clear · clear · very clear

_____   _____   _____   _____

3. Were you given an opportunity to take part in class discussion?

None of the time · Some of the time · Most of the time · All of the time

_____   _____   _____   _____

4. Were the methods of lesson presentation varied?

Not varied · Somewhat varied · Varied · Mostly varied

_____   _____   _____   _____

5. Did the methods of instruction make the lessons interesting?

Not interesting · Somewhat interesting · Interesting · Very interesting

_____   _____   _____   _____

6. Comments (if any):

_____

_____

APPENDIX G

INSTRUCTOR'S EVALUATION OF STUDENT

(Basic Training Outcome Scores)

The instructor completes one on each student; it is to be kept in the student's record. This evaluation is not given to the student. From this evaluation the instructor determines the final score the student receives for the course and whether the student passes the course or not. This evaluation will only be as good as the record kept on each student. If the student is dissatisfied with the outcome received; the instructor will be able to pull this record to show the student, why he or she receives that outcome.

===========

Student Name: _____ Date: _____ Instructor:

_____

1. Student attended all class sessions (Possible score 100). Twenty Point deducted for each day absent. Days absent_____ Days present___ Total attendance Score _____.

2. Student did class assignments (Required reading, conflict profile exercise, watch Luther movie: 100 points for each total possible core 300 points). Required reading score___. Conflict profile score__. Luther movie score___. Total score received_____.

3. Student participate in class discussion:

None (zero point). Moderately (50 to 100 point). Excessively (50 points).

4. Short Quiz Score (10 point total for each quiz of 5 questions correctly answered). Grand total (depends **on how many short quiz were given):** _____.

7. Final Exam Score (total possible points 160) _____. (must receive a minimum of 80 to pass) *

8. Did the Student meet the course objectives: Yes ___ No ___

9. Recommendation: Pass the course ____ Repeats the course: _____

Comments:

_____

_____

*Note: A student may receive high score on everything else but fails the final exam. This means the student repeats the course.

APPENDIX H

CURRICULLUM EVALUATION

Your evaluation of the *Agents of Peace-Managers of Conflict* curriculum helps us improve the course for other students. Please take some time to answer the questions as honestly as possible. Do not write your name on the evaluation; it is anonymous. Drop it in the box at the end of the table when you finish.

Section I: Becoming an Agent of Peace

There are five lessons in this section. Tell us how helpful each lesson in this section was for you. Shade in one circle for each lesson. Add comments in the box below as to how we can best improve a specific lesson or the entire section.

Not Helpful · Somewhat Helpful· Helpful ·Very Helpful

	Not Helpful	Somewhat Helpful	Helpful	Very Helpful
Lesson 1: The need for Plan:	O	O	O	O
Lesson 2: Your Conflict Style:	O	O	O	O
Lesson 3: Your Theology of Conf:	O	O	O	O
Lesson 4: Peace, A Christian Duty:	O	O	O	O
Lesson 5: Why Manage Conflict:	O	O	O	O

Add comments here:

Section II: Understanding the Dynamics of Conflict

Tell us how helpful the lessons in this section were for you. Shade in one circle for each lesson. Add comments in the box below as to how we can improve this section.

Not Helpful· Somewhat Helpful · Helpful ·Very Helpful

	Not Helpful	Somewhat Helpful	Helpful	Very Helpful
Lesson 6: A Strategic Peace Plan:	O	O	O	O
Lesson 7: Biblical Precedence (OT):	O	O	O	O
Lesson 8: Biblical Precedence (NT):	O	O	O	O
Lesson 9: Historical Precedence:	O	O	O	O
Lesson 10: The Nature of Conflict:	O	O	O	O

Add comments here:

Section III: Understanding the Mechanics of Conflict

Tell us how helpful the lessons in this section were for you. Shade in one circle for each lesson. Add comments in the box below as to how we can best improve this section.

Not Helpful· Somewhat Helpful ·Helpful ·Very Helpful

	Not Helpful	Somewhat Helpful	Helpful	Very Helpful
Lesson 11: Causes of Sources:	O	O	O	O
Lesson 12: Gen. peacemaking 1:	O	O	O	O
Lesson 13: Gen. peacemaking-2:	O	O	O	O
Lesson 14: Biblical peace-1	O	O	O	O
Lesson 15: Biblical peace-2	O	O	O	O

Add comments here:

Section IV: Launching A *Resident Council* Peace Ministry at Your Church

Tell us how helpful the lessons in this section were for you. Shade in one circle for each lesson. Add comments in the box below as to how we can improve this section.

Not Helpful · Somewhat Helpful · Helpful · Very Helpful

	Not Helpful	Somewhat Helpful	Helpful	Very Helpful
Lesson 16: Corporate unity	O	O	O	O
Lesson 17: Social media	O	O	O	O
Lesson 18: Pretraining Phase	O	O	O	O
Lesson 19: The Training Phase	O	O	O	O
Lesson 20: Post-training Phase	O	O	O	O

Add comments here:

Thanks, so much for using the Agents of Peace-Masters of Conflict curriculum. Please send feedback to Michael Dewar at: Revdewar@gmail.com.

OTHER BOOKS BY THIS AUTHOR

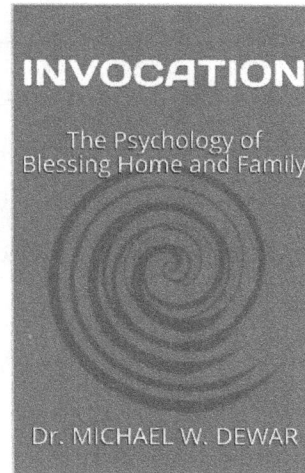

THE BOOK OF LIFE & THE BOOKS OF WRATH — MICHAEL W. DEWAR

THE MASTER LIST UNCOVERED — The Hell-bound Crowd — Michael W. Dewar

BLESS AND CURSE NOT — The Art of Blessing — MICHAEL DEWAR

INVOCATION — The Psychology of Blessing Home and Family — Dr. MICHAEL W. DEWAR

Available at: Amazon.com or at: michaeldewar.com

ABOUT THE AUTHOR

The Reverend Dr. Michael W. Dewar, Sr. is a pastor, Bible teacher, and mentor in the spiritual life for more than thirty-five years. He is a specialist in conflict management and resolution. He provides counsel and consulting to pastors and ministry leaders in resolving conflicted situations and establishing peace ministries in churches.

Rev. Dewar earned the Master of Divinity from Eastern Theological Seminary (now, Palmer Theological Seminary, Eastern University), a Master of Social Work from Wurzweiler, Yeshiva University, and a Doctor of Ministry from Regent University, School of Divinity. He has written several books on the spiritual life. He is founder and pastor of the New York Congregational Baptist Church in Brooklyn. He lives here in New York City with his family.

www.ingramcontent.com/pod-product-compliance
Lightning Source LLC
Chambersburg PA
CBHW081654270326
41933CB00017B/3171